MOVE YOUR CHURCH TO ACTION

MOVE YOUR CHURCH TO ACTION

KENT R. HUNTER

ABINGDON PRESS
Nashville

MOVE YOUR CHURCH TO ACTION

Copyright © 2000 by Abingdon Press

This book is printed on recycled, acid-free, elemental-chlorine–free paper.

Library of Congress Cataloging-in-Publication Data

Hunter, Kent R., 1947–
  Move your church to action / Kent R. Hunter.
    p.   cm.
  ISBN 0-687-03134-6 (alk. paper)
  1. Church renewal. I. Title.
BV600.2.H848 2000
262'.001'7—dc21

99-15046
CIP

Scripture quotations, unless otherwise noted, are from the HOLY BIBLE: NEW INTERNATIONAL VERSION®. Copyright © 1973, 1978, 1984 by the International Bible Society. Used by permission of Zondervan Publishing House. All rights reserved.

Those noted TEV are from The Good News Bible: The Bible in Today's English Version—Old Testament: Copyright © American Bible Society 1976; New Testament: Copyright © American Bible Society 1966, 1971, 1976, 1992.

Those noted KJV are from the King James Version.

00 01 02 03 04 05 06 07 08 09—10 9 8 7 6 5 4 3 2 1

MANUFACTURED IN THE UNITED STATES OF AMERICA

CONTENTS

ACKNOWLEDGMENTS

It is a great privilege to be a part of the reinvigoration that God is bringing to the church. I am honored to have the role of working with churches and helping them become more effective in reaching people for Jesus Christ in this changing world.

God has used a number of people in my life to provide a great influence. Some are relatives, others are mentors and teachers. Each has had a great impact on my thinking and understanding of the church.

I am deeply grateful to God for my father, Robert Hunter, who died when I was in college. Also, I am grateful for my mother, Dolores Licorish, and her special husband, Wallace. I have been blessed with a great and supportive wife, Janet, and two understanding children, Laura and Jonathan.

Among the many great teachers who have influenced my life, I thank God for Vic Halboth, Leroy Biesenthal, Ellis Rottmann, C. Peter Wagner, Donald McGavran, Lyle Schaller, and John Maxwell. I have also been blessed with a great staff and board of directors at The Church Doctor ministries. I am also grateful for our radio partners at Ambassador Advertising Agency, and the many stations that air The Church Doctor as we seek to help churches one Christian at a time. I believe, without any doubt, that you can move your church to action.

"How many church members does it take to change a lightbulb?" The answer: "Who said anything about change?" As the church moves into the twenty-first century, you and I are bombarded in a world characterized by change. Technology is reshaping everything around us. It wasn't that many years ago that no one had e-mail, digital television was a theory, people actually listened to music on something called a "record," and there was an institution that I distinctly remember as a drive-in movie theater.

Change has also affected the church. Not too long ago I read in the *Wall Street Journal* that two decades ago churches bought two hundred and twenty thousand large organs a year to provide music in their sanctuaries. Recent figures show sales down below seventeen thousand a year; and those are in churches often struggling to find someone who knows how to play them. There are other, less obvious changes affecting the church. Many of those adults who rebelled in the 1960s and 1970s raised children without the church. They decided to "let them choose their religion on their own." Those children are now adults, and hundreds of thousands of them have no Christian memory—they do not remember a time when they were a Christian. While well-meaning Christians might hold up a sign at a sports event that says "John 3:16," most unchurched Americans don't have a clue what that refers to. They don't even recognize it as a Bible verse.

The United States has become a mission field. Some believe it is the fifth-largest mission field (in population count) in the world. There are more self-declared unchurched, nonaffiliated people in the United States than in any other country in the world except China, the former Soviet Union, India, and Brazil. *Leadership* magazine reported that while the United States sends more missionaries than any other country, it also receives the second-largest number of missionaries. While the Christian churches in the United States send missionaries beyond the U.S. border to serve on the "mission field," other Christians around the world send, collectively, more missionaries to the United States than are received by any other country in the world except Brazil.

As North America became a mission field, the church, caught in a "business-as-usual" pattern, has failed to see itself as a mission. Christians do not see themselves as missionaries. Most seminaries don't train pastors to be missionaries. Many who plan worship assume whoever walks in the door is going to understand the church lingo. The end result is thousands of churches that are plateaued or declining and millions of Christians who are frustrated by ineffectiveness. Lyle Schaller, in his book *Tattered Trust* (Nashville: Abingdon Press, 1997), has predicted that one thousand to one hundred and fifty thousand congregations will dissolve in the first five decades of the twenty-first century. That averages five to eight a day.

Our research shows that most Christians don't have a clue to what the mission of the church is. As we consulted with congregations and circulated surveys and questionnaires, we discovered that up to 80 percent of church members believe that the primary purpose of the church is to provide a place of fellowship where Christians can share God's love with one another rather than reach out to those who are unchurched. George Barna, in *The Index of Leading Spiritual Indicators* (Nashville: Word Books, 1996), indicates that 80 percent of those who identify themselves as "born-again" Christians couldn't hazard a guess as to what is the meaning of the Great Commission.

Many today are experiencing a holy restlessness in their Christian life and in their church. There are exciting, dynamic, growing churches that dot the landscape. They give us a point of comparison or contrast. Many perceive their own churches to be dull, mediocre, apathetic, and stalled. Some church-shop. Others want change. Still others draw the line and say, "They have changed the rest of my world. They are not going to change my church!" The whole situation is challenged even more by the fact that baby boomers (those born after 1946) are now taking over the power centers of local churches. Their children raised and careers managed, they are taking a more active part in the church. But boomers are a critical bunch who are not afraid to challenge authority and the status quo. This makes for an uncomfortable time for Christians. Yet, it is a time that is abundant with opportunities. It is a time for reshaping and retooling the church. It is a time of transition. It is a time of reformation, renewal, and perhaps even revival.

Someone once said that it takes only one small enthusiastic flea to drive a dog nuts. In churches all across the land, God is using people like you who have a passion and a vision for what the church can be. You can be a catalyst. You can ignite your church and move it to action.

INTRODUCTION

As Dean and Bill walked through the double doors of the educational wing and into the parking lot, they found themselves talking about the board meeting. It had ended early for a change, and perhaps subconsciously they felt that it was too early to go home from a church meeting. As they paused under a street light the conversation turned to a reflection on the recent history of the congregation and its present situation.

"You know," mused Bill as he looked across the empty parking lot, "I can remember not too long ago when the parking lot was almost full every Sunday morning."

"You're right," Dean replied. "It's been several years now since we've had to set up chairs for a worship service."

Bill looked at the ground, as though studying his shoes. "It just seems to me that lately our church has been kind of stuck. You know what I mean? We don't have many new people coming like we did before. We used to have more baptisms."

"It's more than that," replied Dean. "Even the people we do have aren't as active. Attendance is down in Sunday school and adult Bible class. And as Lois was saying tonight at supper, the ladies are getting older; they don't want to work as hard as they used to. They want some of the younger ones to take over, but the younger ones don't seem interested. It's the same for the men. It seems like it's been harder to get people to run for office the past few years."

Dean thought for a moment, then added, "Our church really isn't dying, as I see it. We're just not moving forward. It seems like there's just apathy."

"Yes," replied Bill. "I feel it too. I wish there was a way we could get moving again."

Move Your Church to Action is for people like Dean and Bill. It's for leaders and pastors of churches like those at Dean and Bill's church. It's for congregations that seem, at least in some ways, to be at a standstill or even declining. This book is for people who want to learn how God can use them to move their church off dead center. It's for those who feel called by God to be part of a church that is going and growing. It's also a book for churches that want to avoid getting into a position where there doesn't seem to be any forward motion.

Many churches suffer from what sailboat enthusiasts call "being in irons." The wind moves through the sails, the boat bobs up and down, the sailors are poised intently, but the boat is making no progress. That boat is "in irons." There is no forward motion. It's like a car stuck in a snow-drift; the wheels spin, but there's no forward movement, no progress. Churches "in irons" sport full calendars, numerous board and committee meetings, various programs and activities, but they show no forward direction, no growth.

GROWING CHURCHES

Should a church always be growing? The answer is yes—and that answer is one of the biases of this book. This book assumes that, with few exceptions, God himself planned for the groups of his people gathered to be healthy, to be in motion, to be moving in a growth pattern.

This book also assumes that God wants churches to reflect growth on four levels: (1) *growing up*—"Grow in the grace and knowledge of our Lord and Savior Jesus Christ" (2 Pet. 3:18); (2) *growing together in fellowship*—"Every day they continued to meet together in the temple courts. They broke bread in their homes and ate together" (Acts 2:46); (3) *growing out*—"The Lord added to their number daily those who were being saved" (Acts 2:47); (4) *growing more (church planting)*—"You will be my witnesses . . . to the ends of the earth" (Acts 1:8).

Such growth occurs when God's people individually and collectively express a lifestyle based on the Savior's two great calls. In the first, Jesus calls us to faith and discipleship. This means more than membership. Discipleship means learning, growing, and increasingly following Jesus Christ. In the second call, Jesus summons us to mission, to reach out and share the gospel with others, discipling them into the community of believers. Answering these calls and moving the church to action is not really something that you and I can do. Only God can move the church forward. That's an important principle to remember as we explore how to find the mix that moves your church forward.

Unless the Lord builds the house, the builders build in vain. As the apostle Paul reminds us, the church of Corinth was started when he planted the seed and Apollos watered, but God brought the growth (1 Cor. 3:6). It is God who moves the church forward. But God did so and continues to do so by using people. It's like planting a garden. Only God can bring forth the miracle of life out of a lifeless seed. Yet, for whatever reason, God in his wisdom has decided to work through people. God could grow the garden on his own, but he doesn't. God uses people to plant, cultivate, weed, fertilize, and water.

Likewise, in the church God has great growth on his mind. God wants people to grow up, grow together, grow out, and grow more. He has designed his church around the principles of discipleship and mission. But God has decided to use people to get the job done. From our point of view, that's a tremendous risk. Sometimes people are lazy. Sometimes they get involved in the sins of the flesh. Sometimes they are shortsighted. Sometimes they lack faith in what God can accomplish. Sometimes they resist change. All of these are risks, but they are risks that God himself has assumed, giving people power through his Word and Spirit to accomplish the mission God has sent them to do.

The aim of *Move Your Church to Action* is to help you find the mix of church-life ingredients God intends for your church so that it can become and remain all that God has called it to be. This is not a goal to be "successful," as the world defines it. The issue here is biblical stewardship, management, and effectively using the resources that God has given to us. God has called us to discipleship and to be instruments for discipling others. God has called us to be in mission, sharing that powerful gospel with others. How can we do that most effectively? That is the quest of this book.

Moving a church to action is not a program, an activity, or a gimmick. It is nothing less than spiritual renewal in the hearts and lives of the people gathered around God's message of forgiveness. That's the right mix.

1

THE ACTION CHURCH

This is a great time to be alive in the Christian church. There have been other times in history when exciting things happened, but I wouldn't trade this era for any other even if it included the opportunity to walk with the Lord himself. We live in an age when God is doing marvelous things among Christians.

There are at least seven characteristics that mark this age of the church:

1. *There is a rising interest in the supernatural.* From the cults to the occult, people are searching for meaning in life. Growing, exciting, vibrant Christian churches sense this and help people understand the meaning of life. They bring the Law and the gospel, the cross and the resurrection, to bear on people's lives and help them see not only the way to get to eternity but also how to get through next week.

Sound, clear, biblical teaching is important. But just as important as theology is theology applied. Theology fascinates people, but they also want to know what theology does. People today are receptive to something beyond Christianity in a vacuum. They want theory, but they also want practice. It is a time for action.

2. *There is a growing division between congregations that are active, alive, and involved in quality and quantity growth and those that are not.* This is true among mainline Protestant denominations, independents, and even the Roman Catholic Church. People will search for a congregation that

is "alive." If they don't find one that is part of their own denominational family, they cross denominational lines (in increasing numbers). Church-shopping is a rapidly growing phenomenon. Critics, usually those from declining congregations, complain that church shoppers are looking for entertainment and lack loyalty. This may be true of some, but many of those who move to more active congregations are among the best givers, the most involved, the Bible students, and the active witnesses of their faith. As this phenomenon continues the gap will widen between churches that emphasize personal discipleship (individual growth) and mission (corporate growth) and those that do not.

3. *There is a serious concern for Bible study.* This is especially seen in the networks of small groups that are seeking a "high-touch" Christianity in a high-tech world. Their Bible study is usually inductive. Instead of having a teacher lecture about the Bible, they discover together what the Bible says and what it means for daily living. Bible study often has a greater impact in a relational environment (a small group meeting in a home) than in the institutional environment (a class at the church). This emphasis on Bible study is enhanced by contemporary Bible translations and study materials. A growing number of long-term Bible study programs are available to those who want an in-depth exposure to the Scriptures. This serious concern for Bible study is a central key to the health and vitality of a church that wants to move into action. Churches don't grow unless Christian people grow. Christian people don't grow unless they are involved in the Word of God. Bible study is the hub around which the twin aspects of discipleship and mission revolve.

4. *There is an ever-increasing degree of scrutiny in the church.* Members are more prone to be concerned about the effectiveness of programs and activities in the church. There is a pursuit of excellence growing among Christians. Many are no longer willing to accept mediocrity as the norm. This trend may result in landscaping around the church, carpet-

ing for the sanctuary, serious evaluation of an evangelism program, a careful review of the Sunday school curriculum, job descriptions for congregational leaders, pressure on the pastor to perform, and a demand on the denomination for relevant programming.

5. *Laypeople are increasingly getting involved in ministry.* Previously, any time groups got together around the church they looked to the pastor to lead them in prayer. Now laypeople are increasingly leading prayer. They are also making hospital visits, ministering in nursing homes, witnessing their faith, leading home Bible studies, and caring for the needy. The involvement of the laity has often paralleled the rediscovery of spiritual gifts. The biblical study of spiritual gifts results in a healthy release of individuals for ministry. As people study about spiritual gifts they learn that (1) the church is a living organism; (2) each Christian is an important part of that organism; (3) Jesus Christ is at the head and in control; (4) each person has a unique function that God has designed for the sake of the Body; and (5) the whole Body is healthy and grows when each part functions as it should.

6. *There are a growing number of alternative ways in which congregations can support missionary activity.* Many churches engage in personalized mission support, making direct contact with their missionaries. This contrasts with traditional methods that funnel support through a denominational board or commission. Many congregations are involved in both forms of support.

The number of task-oriented agencies is growing. These agencies are oriented toward meeting particular needs. They provide a healthy ministry to complement denominational boards and committees. Some examples are Bible translators, missionary airplane pilots, church growth agencies, youth ministry agencies, women's ministries, ministries that provide evangelism materials, and church consultation agencies.

7. *There is more missionary activity in the world than ever before.* There are more missionaries today than at any time in history. Many middle-aged Christians are seeking ministry-related second careers. Particularly in the Western part of the world, many people have tasted success but long for significance. They want to make an impact. They want to make a difference. Some volunteer more at their church. Some end up on staff. Others train for the mission field. They represent an army that God is raising up. They bring their experience and knowledge to ministry. Many are taking a careerful of skills to the mission field.

There is another growing phenomenon in missionary endeavors. Missionaries, once sent primarily from certain Western countries to the rest of the world, are now sent from every continent to every other continent. African churches now send missionaries to the United States. Mass media are having an enormous effect on the number of people hearing the gospel on a regular basis. At the turn of the century there was no television or radio. Today 1.2 billion people see or hear a Christian broadcast at least once each month.

It's an exciting time to be a part of the Christian church. But how did we get here? From where have we come? In many ways the Christian movement has come full circle to a New Testament position of action. Let's trace this theme by looking at the church's history in a brief interpretive overview.

THE NEW TESTAMENT CHURCH

In Acts 1:8, Luke records Jesus' last words to his closest disciples just before Jesus ascended to rulership of the universe. He said, "You will receive power when the Holy Spirit comes on you; and you will be my witnesses in Jerusalem, and in all Judea and Samaria, and to the ends of the earth." These parting words summarize Jesus' mission and vision and the purpose for which he discipled his followers. His clear intention and goal was that the church continue in his mission—the mission for which he bled and died. The words of Acts 1:8 also point toward the birth of his church. In Acts 2, a magnificent historical event multiplied Christ's band of disciples into multitudes who would take the gospel to every corner of the world for centuries to come. The church at Pentecost, the fledgling Body of Christ, exhibited a number of characteristics:

1. *Dreamers and visionaries moved the church.* This was an age when the Spirit was poured out (Joel 2:28; Acts 2:17). The New Testament people, filled with the living Lord, would face hostile councils and threatening emperors as they proclaimed the message. They encountered dangers as they followed big dreams and pursued enormous visions of evangelizing the world. They were people on God's worldwide mission.

2. *The New Testament church was characterized by power and boldness.* These people demonstrated power from on high and were bold in their proclamation to friends, relatives, foreigners, and enemies (Acts 4:29). Their words and lives testified to their faith in Christ. They learned how to do all things in Christ who empowered them. And God accompanied the preaching of the gospel with signs and wonders, doing new things through normal people as God waged war with the principalities and powers (1 Cor. 15:25).

3. *The people shared in the passion of the mission.* They had contagious passion for lost humanity, based on the top priority to reach people for Jesus Christ. They were ready and eager to share their new life in Christ and bring others to the gospel (Acts 8:1, 4). The apostle Paul summarized their worldview by saying that he would become all things to all people so that by any means some might be saved (1 Cor. 9:22). The believers displayed tenacious perseverance, reflecting a willingness to give their lives as witnesses to the

person of Jesus Christ for the salvation of those who did not know him.

4. *Mission and risk characterized their work.* The faithful were so overwhelmed by their commission to make disciples of all nations that they were literally out of control—human control. Rarely did they seek to control the church. They moved on to new territories at the impulse of the Spirit. They began new churches and left them in the hands of new converts. They were neither concerned with bureaucracies nor preoccupied with voting. They were more concerned about praying, teaching, sharing, fellowshipping, gathering for praise, and sharing in the body and blood of Jesus Christ as they celebrated their unity in forgiveness through the power of the cross. They knew that the head of the church was not the pastor, a council, a pope, a board, or any individual. They spoke of Jesus Christ as Head. They weren't following tradition; they were making history. Most of all, they were making disciples.

5. *Servant leaders distinguished the enterprise.* Following the design of their Master, these leaders were empowering, equipping, and releasing others for ministry. The apostle Paul spoke to the people and encouraged them not to be conformed to this world but to be transformed by the renewal of their minds (Rom. 12:2). The leadership reflected a vision for change—real change, revolutionary change. When people were introduced to Jesus Christ, they became radically different. When cities and empires were infected with the Christian gospel, they ultimately became different political entities. The people of the New Testament were not primarily interested in social change on the surface. They zeroed in on change of the heart, knowing that a change of the heart would address the real problems of people, not just the symptoms. They knew that, in time, this change of heart would bring about real change in social justice and social systems under divine, not human, control.

These same characteristics and powers are available to the church of today, and work wherever the Lord is present and active within his Body. Yet already within the New Testament era leaders fell away, congregations grew discouraged, and factions formed. Paul's letters to the Corinthians and Galatians and John's comments to the seven churches of Asia (Revelation 2–3) will keep us from creating a utopian vision of the New Testament church. Yet through toil and tribulation, conflict and opposition, the good news spread throughout the world, and the mission of Jesus Christ was carried forward with joy and power.

THE CHURCH OF THE MIDDLE AGES

As the centuries passed, the Word of the Lord continued to grow. Lives were blessed and consciences comforted, but problems also increased. The maintenance of church organization and the struggle for church control often turned much of the church's energy away from mission and outreach. Self-centered organizational activity, dedication to traditions, ecclesiastical politics, and authoritarian leadership brought fossilization and lethargy to the church in many places. Intended to be salt, the church took on much of the flavor of the world.

Yet, in the period from 500 to 1500 A.D., the gospel was brought to many non-Christian nations or peoples, often through the work of "professionals" in monastic orders. The message may at times have been a mixture of true reconciliation in Christ and works-righteousness, but the gospel still saved people despite being mixed with falsehood and despite the coercive and conformist methods used by the ecclesiastical systems of the day.

THE REFORMATION CHURCH

The Reformation movement of the sixteenth century, as it reacted to the fossilized and false elements of the medieval church, did much to restore the vision, the joy, and the bold-ness of the New Testament era. The centrality of the gospel of Jesus, peace for troubled consciences, and the joy of salvation brought transforming power into the lives of many. The reformers stood before emperors and kings, risking their lives so that the message could go out. We are in debt to their work, defense, and proclamation of the gospel. But their legacy has often been fossilized, turned into a permanent reaction against something rather than a mission moving forward. The gospel of Jesus Christ, which empowered the church of the New Testament and the church of the Reformation, can be left unused and cold as a rote creed, a forgotten catechism, or a closed Bible. Those who are heirs of the Reformation inher-it also the danger of becoming churches of reaction today.

THE "ACTIONARY" CHURCH

Our lifetime is an age of action, discipleship, and mission for the Body of Christ. The seeds planted in us by the mes-sage of Jesus Christ are blossoming and bearing fruit. The great post-Reformation revivals and missionary move-ments of the past centuries spread the gospel worldwide. The Christian church grew at an increasing rate in the eigh-teenth and nineteenth centuries, outstripping the growth of the world's population. That growth rate slowed in this century as the world population has soared. Yet the Lord, who has given us a great challenge in his Great Commis-sion, gives us the resources and opportunities to work. Our era is still the era of the New Testament, still the age of the Reformation. Today is the day of the Great Commission. Ours is the age for completing the challenge our Lord gave at his ascension. It is the time to make disciples of all peo-ple. Ours is the exciting day of the "actionary" church. Sometimes called new apostolic Reformation churches, these actionary churches have several characteristics.

1. *Servant leaders lead the actionary church.* Servant leaders emerge from the grass roots. They create new power centers for moving the Christian movement forward. They are teachers, writers, and equippers (see chapter 5).

2. *The actionary church is marked by a refocus on practice.* Where the Reformation planted the seeds through theology and theory, the age of action centers on the practice of taking the gospel out to the world. Pure doctrine was the primary concern of the Reformation—and creating solid disciples. It is a means to an end rather than an end in itself. At the time of the Reformation the challenge was to defend the truth. In the age of action the priority is to take that truth of the Reformation, which is the New Testament truth of Jesus Christ, and to share it.

3. *Accountability for world evangelization permeates the mood of the actionary church.* Measurable self-assessment characterizes actionary churches as they seek to perceive and discern the effectiveness of their work of making disciples, multiplying disciples, multiplying churches, and building the Kingdom. God is not measured, but what God's people do with the gospel and how unbelievers respond are measured. "Success" comes not as a result of good administration but as a result of God's activity through his Word; yet self-analysis and accountability help aim and support our human efforts at spreading the gospel.

4. *Mission and risk describe the commitment of the actionary church.* Once again the church is out of control, humanly speaking. The age of action is a grassroots movement that progresses from the bottom up. It is an age in which God is calling forth dreamers and visionaries who are enlightened by Word and Spirit and characterized by boldness. The church's evangelistic passion endures with a tenacity that sustains its leaders beyond the challenges of mediocrity and "business as usual." This is the age of action.

How does a congregation move into the age of action? How does a church become a part of this growing Christian movement in this exciting era of history? It happens just like fire spreads from one object to another. God's Spirit, through his living, powerful Word, ignites a vision for discipleship and mission in each person. As individuals gather together and see God's will more clearly, a congregation takes on a new personality. As spiritual renewal of the church happens through the joy and power of God's Word, the church moves into action, removing barriers and reviving the vision. Vision follows renewal.

Sometimes we have to see things differently in order to do things differently. One of my favorite stories was told by my good friend Lyle Schaller when he was training me as a church consultant years ago: A man was looking out his living-room window. He saw that it was a beautiful day outside and yelled to his wife, who was at the other end of the house, "Dear, it's a beautiful day outside. Why don't we go out and get some exercise?"

His wife, who was washing dishes in the kitchen, looked out the window and saw that it was indeed a beautiful day. She yelled back across the house to her husband, "Yes, dear, it is a beautiful day. Why don't you go upstairs and change your clothes and go outside. When I finish the dishes here, I'll go upstairs and change my clothes. Then I'll meet you outside, and we'll get some exercise."

As he looked out the living-room window, he saw the tennis courts across the road. But as she looked out the kitchen window, she saw the swimming pool in the backyard. After they had changed clothes and met outside, they discovered they were dressed very differently.

The window through which we see life has a tremendous impact on our behavior. If you want to move your church forward, you'll have to deal with that window on the world through which people are looking. That process begins by taking a look at your church and determining its nature. It's time for a checkup for the Body of Christ.

Discussion Questions

1. Discuss whether this is a great time to be alive in the Christian church.

2. Evaluate the seven characteristics that mark this age of the church from the standpoint of yourself and your congregation. Which are valid for you? Which are not valid?

3. In the context of your heritage and theology, is the prototype described as "the New Testament church" one you can visualize as appropriate for your congregation today?

4. Compare the New Testament and actionary churches. Are they the same, or are there significant differences that you can identify?

5. Consider how you may lead your church from how you now perceive it to another view consistent with your evaluation of the present age and demands of the Scripture. List potential roadblocks to this move.

2

TIME FOR A CHECKUP

After the New Year's Eve service, Dan and George were standing at the table in the hallway just outside the sanctuary. They were looking at all the contribution envelopes for the next year that hadn't been picked up by members of the congregation.

"You know," said George, "only about one-third of the members of this congregation are actively involved in the church. There's another third you never see. They aren't involved, they never give, and they don't attend except for some who come at Christmas and Easter."

"I think that's true," said Dan. "And there's a middle third that's sort of in-between. About half of those worship with some regularity, and the other half only worship occasionally. It seems like our church is very unhealthy."

For hundreds of churches like Dan and George's, "unhealthy" may not be the only fit description. "Typical" might be appropriate as well. Although it is not acceptable for the Body of Christ, it is common for congregations to reflect these symptoms. This has several important implications for diagnosing problems in your church.

First, what is the size of your church? Many churches are compared with others by the number of members on the rolls. Church consultants never analyze churches that way. Some churches do present an accurate picture when they report membership. Others have people on the rolls they haven't seen in twenty years.

I was in a church once where we discovered that several members listed on the rolls were deceased. The church was in a state of decline and denial. An inaccurate roll is common for a declining church, and it makes a comparison of size based on membership almost useless.

The most accurate way to determine the size of your church is by recording average worship attendance. (Shut-in or homebound and institutionalized members need to be included in this figure as well.) The information can be further refined by subtracting the number of children in the service from the average worship attendance.

A second implication is that if you have about one-third of the "core" membership doing most of the work and giving most of the money, usually about two-thirds of the income, your church is fairly typical.

The third implication is that the one-third core group usually sets the pace, the tone, and the direction of the church. The views and attitudes of this group will shape the future of the congregation.

Church analysis focuses on the core group. But diagnosing the health and vitality of the church's core group is not simply a sociological or psychological exercise. It includes the spiritual condition of the church. Are the members spiritually healthy, maturing, and growing in discipleship? Do they participate in Bible study? Are they regular in their communion attendance? Do their lives reflect God's will?

Do the people of the church generally show the presence of the fruit of the Spirit: love, joy, peace, patience, kindness, goodness, faithfulness, humility, and self-control? Is the compassion of Christ apparent in their lives? Do they care about those who are hurting, in need, and suffering? Are they concerned that others know forgiveness through Jesus Christ? Is there mutual discipline in the fellowship of believers? Is there a real concern for worldwide evangelization?

Moving the church into action begins with church analysis and diagnosis of the general health of the church. Six areas of analysis are helpful:

1. Mission or Maintenance?
2. Sensitive or Self-Centered?
3. Risk or Rut?
4. Progressive or Petrified?
5. Planned or Pasteurized?
6. Organized or Ossified?

MISSION OR MAINTENANCE?

In the city of Merrysville, there are two churches of the same denomination. They are about the same size in membership. Both are made up of middle-class people. Trinity is on the east side of Merrysville, and St. Paul is on the west. Both churches are considering taking on a financial challenge of $50,000.

At St. Paul, the long-range planning committee has discovered the enormous potential that the church has for reaching unchurched people in its immediate area. But the pastor is already overworked, and the evangelism committee needs some professional guidance and leadership. The long-range planning committee has recommended that the congregation call a director of evangelism for about $50,000. This would be the total cost to the congregation for a professional church worker with expertise in the area of evangelism. This person would train and equip members of the church to share their faith more effectively. This person would also be in charge of developing an outreach mentality in the congregation.

Across town, the members of Trinity are faced with a $50,000 challenge as well. The company that services the pipe organ has indicated that the instrument is quite old and in need of major repairs. It could break down at any time. The congregation could buy a new organ, but it would cost well over $100,000 for an instrument equal in quality to the present one. The other option is to rebuild the organ, which the company indicates would cost about $50,000. The music and worship committee has approached the congregation with the recommendation that they begin a fund-raising activity to collect $50,000 to rebuild the organ as soon as possible.

To a large degree, the success of the proposals at St. Paul and at Trinity will be based on the mission or maintenance mentality of the congregations. In most churches, the probability of Trinity rebuilding the organ is much greater than the probability of St. Paul calling an evangelist. Many churches have lost the vision for their mission. They have settled into a maintenance mentality, and for many members, maintaining the institution is the mission of the church.

The word *mission* is not in the Bible. But the idea of mission is what the Bible is all about. *Mission* means "being sent." From Genesis to Revelation, the Bible talks about God sending his love and forgiveness in the person of his chosen one, Jesus Christ—the Savior of humanity. Jesus was "sent" by God. He was God's Son, a man on a mission.

Many Christian churches have an Old Testament style of mission. In the Old Testament, Israel was to be a light to the nations. Their history was a story of the kingdom of God breaking into the world of nations. Their triumph showed God's triumph. It served as a warning and an invitation to the nations, a sign of God's presence among them. The people of the nations were to "come" to Israel to see God's forgiving presence among his chosen people.

In the New Testament church, the people of God were commanded to "go." In the Old Testament, God's mission plan was to prepare the world for the Messiah. In the New Testament, God's Messiah is sent to the people, and God in turn sends his people on a mission. Jesus was clear about this mission. He was sent to seek and to save the lost. After his resurrection, he said to his disciples, "As the Father has sent me, I am sending you" (John 20:21). In Matthew 28, Jesus speaks the words of what has become known as the Great Commission. He tells his people to "go and make disciples." Elsewhere, Jesus tells his people to "go into all the world and preach the good news to all creation" (Mark 16:15; see also 13:10). At his ascension, Jesus speaks his last words to the disciples and tells them to be witnesses in Jerusalem (their hometown), Judea (the surrounding area), Samaria (cross-culturally), and to the ends of the earth (the world) (Acts 1:8). Obviously, his people can't be witnesses to the ends of the earth without having a "go" mentality. Unfortunately, many churches reflect a "come" mentality. This is often an indication of too much emphasis on maintenance and not enough stress on mission.

To be healthy, every church must have both mission and maintenance. The issue here is not an either-or question. It's a matter of priorities and emphases. It is a matter of means and ends. What are the means and what is the end? Maintenance is to be a means toward the end of mission. But sometimes maintenance becomes an end in itself.

This is reflected in the *historical maintenance syndrome* of many churches. Many congregations begin with a great mission orientation. A few families gather together seeking to begin a church in a certain area. Perhaps a denominational agency or mission organization sends a church planter into an area to gather such people. As these people assemble, there is a strong inclination toward establishing a church. They give high priority to inviting new people.

The mission mentality takes concrete form in newspaper advertisements, neighborhood canvasses, word-of-mouth invitations, and extensive evangelistic activity. As a church is established, the need for a permanent place to meet grows. The group must establish a permanence in the community. During the first phase of land purchases and building, the mission mentality is quite strong. But as the church builds additions or moves to a larger facility, it often enters the historical maintenance syndrome. Much of the attention, money, and energy of key people in the congregation is funneled toward the building. At this phase in the life of the congregation, the pastor either changes the focus of ministry, or the church changes pastors and calls someone with a "we are here—come to us" mentality.

A parallel phenomenon takes place in this historical maintenance syndrome. During the mission phase of the congregation, many of the members have young children. As the children grow and become the potential young leaders of the church in the next generation, they often do not carry the pioneering spirit—the mission zeal—of their parents. For them, growing up in the church just happened naturally. Their parents were members of the church, and the children were brought to the church. Subconsciously, these second-generation people think that the church grows primarily as people bring their children to church. After all, that is how it happened for them. This parallel phenomenon often contributes to the maintenance mentality of the church.

Mission and maintenance priorities can be diagnosed in a church by looking at the annual budget. How much is spent for mission? How much is spent for maintenance? Even more significant, how much is spent this year compared with last year and the year before that and each of the previous ten to fifteen years? The important issue is not so much the amount but the trend.

How do you move a church that is caught in the historical maintenance syndrome into action? There are three options:

1. *Develop a preventive strategy.* This option is for congregations that are in a mission stance right now and want to remain in that orientation. Don't overbuild. Make sure that

what you build is functional. Don't get yourself deep in debt. Although it varies according to the economic levels of the members of the congregation, this is a good rule of thumb: Do not take on a debt that equals more than two times the giving of the average giving unit, multiplied by the number of units. In other words, if a congregation has 200 giving units and the annual average giving per unit is $400, two times $400 equals $800. Eight hundred dollars multiplied by 200 giving units equals $160,000. This would be the limit of any building extension, renovation, or land expansion project. If the building project would require $200,000, for example, the congregation would have to have $40,000 in cash before it would take on that debt load. But this cash amount should not (under ordinary circumstances) be more than half of the amount to be borrowed. These limitations are designed to restrain the congregation from building something that costs too much to maintain. Such preventive disciplines will help the congregation build something that is practical and viable within the bounds of a properly balanced mission-maintenance budget. The intent is to keep the total of the debt-service load (and annual maintenance cost of the buildings) low enough so that they do not become a priority of the church.

When building, it is important to build for the practitioner, not for the architect. I have met many wonderful architects who do great service for the church. But many architects are more interested in building monuments than missions. Even those who design many churches often do not have a sense of the mission of the church. Many times the first question members of churches ask as they approach an architect is "How much will it cost?" A more important question is "What do you see as the main purpose of the church?" The answer to that question will determine the perspective from which the architect designs the structure.

But what if the church is already in a maintenance pattern? What can be done? There are two remaining options.

2. *Build a missionary spirit within the church.* God can change the attitudes of people, and that in turn will change the mission or maintenance priorities of the church. But as Jesus warned, before you build a tower, sit down and count the cost (Luke 14:28). If you want to build a missionary spirit in your church, plan for a long-term effort, probably at least five years. Attitudes don't change overnight. Attitudinal change takes effort, communication, and time. Make the mission of the church the top priority. Emphasize the importance of growing into discipleship and reaching out to make more disciples. Talk about the purpose of the church. Communicate over and over again that the mission of the church is to grow up, grow together, grow out, and grow more. See that the preaching, the teaching, and the activities of the church emphasize the mission. Scrutinize the budget in terms of the amount of energy and time used by the pastor and church leaders in the areas of mission and maintenance.

In a growing church, work intentionally with the new members. Whether those new members are children of existing members, transfers from other churches, or new Christians, it is important to indoctrinate them (in the positive sense) with the mission and purpose of the church. Be honest with them and tell them that not all members of the church share that vision. Otherwise they will get discouraged or possibly be infected by some of the maintenance attitudes.

When adding new staff, be sure that they share the same vision for mission. Encourage the leaders of the church who have the vision for mission. Sometimes well-meaning Christians have been in positions of leadership for so long that they represent not only old blood but tired blood. New leaders with new blood often need to infiltrate decision-making groups.

The best way to change old-guard thinking is not by

academic teaching, but by experiential learning. In other words, it is important to tell, preach, and teach, but the best way for people to catch the vision for mission is to experience it. Books and films about growing churches can be good. But the best way to experience a missionary spirit is to visit healthy, vital, growing churches. When a pastor has a free Sunday, a visit to the fastest-growing church around should be made. At least once a year the pastor and the key leaders of the congregation should take a field trip to a fast-growing church. Immediately after attending a worship service, the pastor should lead the people in a debriefing of the experience, summarizing aspects of church life that would not be appropriate for their church and listing features that could be adapted effectively to help generate a mission mentality in their own congregation. Besides learning the programs and techniques, the leaders will catch the missionary mentality.

Sometimes, however, it appears that a church has been declining for so long and is so near death that it's impossible to muster the strength and energy to build a missionary spirit. Sometimes in a changing neighborhood cultural differences such as a different language provide significant roadblocks to building a missionary spirit in a church. What can be done? This is option number three.

3. *Plant new mission churches.* This can be accomplished with options one or two, or it can be an alternative option. When a congregation is too old, too tired, or too weak to build a significant spirit, or when it is faced with a need to change to the culture of a new surrounding community, one of the best alternatives is to plant new mission churches. This is based on the important principle that it's easier to give birth than to raise the dead. God's kingdom grows the fastest by planting new churches. This can also rekindle the mission spirit before the church enters the historical maintenance syndrome.

There are several new ways to start churches. They can

begin when new people in the community have a mission mentality and want to branch out in a certain locality or among people of a certain culture group within the neighborhood. A church can begin with people who are already members of the church but want to break off and start new work. Funds can be directed to a missionary agency or a denominational group that can start a church. Whatever strategy is used, it is essential to begin with the people who have the proper mentality and balance toward mission and maintenance.

SENSITIVE OR SELF-CENTERED?

The issue is sensitivity to people. What is most important for your church: the building? proper teaching? programs? What about people?

A study of Jesus and his earthly ministry reveals a strong sensitivity to people. Jesus called all kinds of people, including prostitutes, tax collectors, fishers, and thieves. He was sensitive to people's needs—feeding the hungry, bringing sight to the blind, cleansing lepers, sharing kindness with the lonely, and giving hope to the poor. He accepted people where they were—the woman at the well, Zacchaeus in the tree, and Peter on the water. Jesus was also sensitive to the religious institution of the day. He was aware of the narrowness of the Pharisees. He understood what had happened to bring about a lifeless, solidified religion of rules and regulations. He chose his words carefully in order to meet the Pharisees' need to be challenged to the depths of their religiosity.

Is your church sensitive to the needs of the people? One of the fastest-growing population groups in the United States is the elderly. As we enter the twenty-first century the number of people over the age of sixty-five in the United States will exceed the entire population of Canada. With improvements in medical technology, people live much longer. If your church is in an area with a growing senior citizen population, what are the implications for people sensitivity? Does your church have steps or ramps? Are toilets accessible for wheelchairs? Are they near the sanctuary?

One of the symbols of sensitivity in the church today is the nursery. Churches that don't provide a nursery are not sensitive to young couples. Or, what about nurseries located far away from the sanctuary? Churches with nurseries painted in pastel colors are sensitive to the needs of parents of the 1950s, not modern parents. Churches in middle-class or upper-class areas that expect mothers to volunteer for the nursery aren't sensitive to the lifestyles of young couples in today's world. Each generation represents a different lifestyle with different needs. Is your church sensitive to the needs of today or the needs of several decades ago?

Sensitivity to people and their needs is part of the mix that can lead to innovation and move the church forward. For example, the traditional women's group is often a declining, discouraged, and frustrated gathering of elderly women who love the Lord and are committed to their church but do not understand why they see the demise of their group on the horizon. Sometimes they are angry at the younger women who "don't do their part." The real issue is that the church has not been sensitive to women who represent younger generations.

Traditionally women's groups have been organized to provide an opportunity for women to socialize. The opportunity to come to church and visit with friends and neighbors was a highlight in their lives. Since there wasn't much opportunity to talk at church on Sunday, this group provided a chance to hear the local news.

What has changed? What has brought about the demise of the women's group organized around the socializing principle? The telephone! Younger women, raised with the telephone as the primary source of information, no longer feel a need to meet to find out what's going on. Many women are busy in the workforce. They socialize at work. So women's groups organized around the socializing principle just don't meet a need anymore.

Healthy, vital, and expanding women's groups are usually organized around task-oriented purposes. The women come together specifically for ministry or for intensive Bible study, prayer, and intimate fellowship. The point of this example is not so much how to organize women's groups but to recognize that a congregation sensitive to people will be more likely to scratch where people are itching.

Is your congregation sensitive to outsiders? If the parking lot is full at peak times like Christmas Eve or Easter morning, do you provide parking attendants to help the outsider find a place to park? Are there signs to the restrooms that the visitor can read? Are your bulletin, hymnal, and order of worship geared to helping the visitor? Many churches have reserved parking for the pastor, the organist, the church secretary, and perhaps a few others, but they don't have reserved parking for visitors. In many churches you can't find the restrooms unless you ask someone. This is embarrassing and uncomfortable for a guest. In many churches the order of worship is a combination of a juggling act when using the hymnal, a Bible, and a bulletin; an adventure in sign language, as the clergy gives hand signals to stand, sit, pray, and pay; and a foreign language course using "in house" words like *kyrie, blessed, narthex,* and *offertory.*

How can you move your church to action to become a more sensitive church? One of the best ways to become sensitive to visitors is to become one. If you have not been a visitor at a church for a long time, you owe it to yourself to find the closest church that is the most different from your own. When you attend that church, don't go with anyone from that church. Go by yourself. Experience what it's like to look for a parking spot. Recognize the anxiety of whether you are dressed properly or whether you are entering through the right door. Consider the issue of whether you should have a Bible in your hand or whether you'll be put on the spot or embarrassed at some point in the service. Every Christian ought to have a refresher course at least once a year on what it means to be a visitor. Part of the move toward sensitivity is simply giving the leadership the time it needs to stop and reflect on the needs of the people. Leaders need to take inventory of what the church is doing, whom it is reaching, and whom it is not reaching.

Listening to the needs of the people in your community produces dividends. How do you find out what their needs are? Ask them! One of the best sensitivity-building exercises is to ask a group of people from your church to canvass a random sample of houses in your community. Ask "What could a church do to help people around here?" It's amazing what people will tell you if you listen.

Remember the mission style that Jesus had: He came not to be served but to serve. That mentality will direct your sensitivity to the needs of others. Remember the cross. It is a reminder of the extent to which Christ went to save humanity. Jesus said that his disciples should take up their crosses and follow him. Following him in that mission means being sensitive to the needs of people. The primary need that any person has is to be restored to God by the grace of God in Jesus Christ. That's the good news we have to share.

Risk or Rut?

One of the key areas of diagnosis for moving your church to action is the level of risk reflected by the ministry of your church. Remember, the New Testament church was marked by a boldness and willingness to risk. Is your church risk oriented? Does your church naturally have a pioneering spirit, a bold faith that responds to God's call? There are understandable reasons why churches take on a nonrisk posture. Sometimes it reflects the type of people who are leading the church.

You can generally find three types of attitudes toward risk in a church, and they are sometimes determined by when people were born. One group in the church is made up of the people who lived through the Great Depression. Anyone who has lived through that (or a personal catastrophic event similar to it) has a different worldview from people who have never lived through such an experience. These people are generally more conservative financially and spend their money more carefully. They provide a good balance for those who were born after 1950, some of whom have moved beyond faith to irresponsible stewardship. Sometimes people who lived through the Depression make up a majority of the congregation and are the opinion-makers and leaders of the church. Without a proper understanding of risk and bold faith, they can freeze the church in a nonprogressive stance.

A second group consists of those born after the Depression and who lived through World War II. They did not experience the trauma of the Depression, but these people are cautious even though they are much more risk oriented than those who lived through the Depression. They are more willing to try new programs. They are more likely to vote for the new computer in the church office, as long as the computer committee has done its homework thoroughly and provides all the facts for intelligent decision making.

The third group, born after World War II, includes many with a credit-card mentality who are prone to live beyond their means, as well as many others who have an optimistic, positive outlook on life and are much more willing to move forward with innovations in the church. They are also less likely to have institutional or denominational loyalties.

They aren't hung up on worn-out traditions or yesterday's programs.

There are, of course, exceptions to these categories of people. Nevertheless, identifying where people are coming from helps to understand their relative openness to risk and boldness and how they will respond to innovation and change.

There needs to be a good balance between risk and caution, but churches are inclined to have nonrisk postures. This is interesting, since the New Testament church was distinguished by risk and boldness. It is also challenging because faith requires risk to a certain degree. It is not risk with the absence of caution, but it is an intelligent risk trusting God for the impossible. In a fascinating way, nonrisk attitudes show up dramatically around the subject of money.

Many churches, when discussing the possibility of taking on a debt for ministry, a building, or land, will debate for hours about a debt that seems so large. But when it is broken down, the per capita debt is usually so low that it is minuscule in comparison to the personal debt load most of the people carry on their houses, cars, or businesses.

It is indeed sinful to take on irresponsible debt, but the opposite extreme is more prevalent. People are less willing to take on their personal share of a corporate debt in the church than they are to assume a debt in their personal lives. Sometimes this reflects that they have more faith in themselves and their ability to pay off a debt than they do in God, who is the provider of all things. When it comes to risk, the congregational conversation too often centers around "what we can afford." But if the congregation functions entirely on what it can afford, it has not entered the realm of faith. The writer of Hebrews says, "Faith is being sure of what we hope for and certain of what we do not see" (11:1). If we are basing our decisions and actions only on what we can see, we have yet to enter the realm of faith. We are simply doing business as any secular person or corporate group. In essence, this is not a church (corporate) problem; it is an individual faith problem and needs to be addressed as such.

Money is perhaps the most dismal aspect of church life connected to the issue of risk versus rut. But it's not the only area. Congregations are often afraid to start new programs. This fear is rarely discussed, but it is a latent uncertainty among many people. The unwillingness to risk and start new programs, especially among new leaders, often lies in the fear that the programs might fail.

The church climate is important at this point. There must be a climate in which there is permission to fail and therefore permission to try. Church leaders need to talk openly about the possibility of the failure of new programs. They need to establish a precedent for a willingness to try, and they must support those who try something and fail. New programs shouldn't be taken too seriously. It's not a sin to try and fail. But it can be a sin not to try. Many churches are not involved in long-range goal-setting because they are afraid the goals may change with the passage of time. The congregation simply needs permission to change its goals. It needs to understand that a future revision of its goals does not lessen their current value. Those goals get the church down the road to a certain point. At that point the congregation may change the destination, but at least the goals helped the people advance that far. Without those goals, the church might have taken a different turn and ended up on a wrong path. How do you move your church to action toward responsible risk?

1. *Discuss the faith issues connected with risk.* When people discuss a new program or the expenditure of money, human aspects of the issue are discussed thoroughly. That's fine, but what about the faith issues? Get to the heart of the matter. Does God want us to do this? Is this within God's will? Is this God's timing? Is this the way God would have us move forward?

2. *Don't let people say that it's a matter of not enough money unless that is true.* Rather than not enough money, the issue is usually not enough giving. Always break financial issues down into per capita cost. Emphasize that the church is the Body of Christ, not an institution. The Body is made up of many members. When counting per capita cost, don't count every member of the church. Babies usually don't give much. Count as active-giving units the average number of adults in church in an average week.

3. *When discussing a new expenditure, identify the element of faith that goes beyond what you can afford or what you can understand.* What part of the issue is identified with trust in God?

4. *Give yourself permission to fail and therefore permission to try.* Give yourself permission to laugh at yourself as a congregation. Create an atmosphere in which you can say "Well, we tried that. It didn't work, but we learned from it." Recognize that it is more important to try and fail—and to learn—than it is not to try at all.

5. *Celebrate victories.* When you risk and trust God for what is possible, when you have tried new programs or spent money wisely, give thanks and praise to God and to the people for their trust in God. Many congregations don't risk because they never celebrate victories, and their risk-taking is not positively reinforced. Boast (with personal humility) about what God has done and can do through you as a congregation. Paul did (2 Cor. 8:1-7).

Progressive or Petrified?

How relevant is your church? In the Christian church, theology is sometimes confused with practice. Theology doesn't change because God doesn't change. God's Word doesn't change. But everything else does. In fact, God changes people. God's Word changes societies and cultures.

In the Scriptures, God uses the most radical words and concepts to describe the extent of change experienced by a person who becomes a Christian. For human beings, the most radical changes are birth and death. These are the terms that God uses to explain the transformation that occurs in a person who is in Christ. The Bible talks about the death of the Old Adam, about being "born again," about new life in Jesus Christ. That is radical change. Consequently, the church should be the most progressive group of people on earth. But it isn't. The primary reason is that sometimes Christians confuse theology with practice.

When Jesus entered this world, he was born as a human being and walked this earth like one of us. He ate. He slept. He worked, sweat, cried, and eventually died. He spoke the language of the people. He dressed like the people. He used concepts and stories that they could understand. That God came in the person of Jesus Christ is called the incarnation, meaning that God came "in the flesh." It is God's ultimate statement that he wants his mission to be relevant. He is still the God of history. He is the God of Abraham, Isaac, and Jacob, and he is also contemporary with you and me. But some twenty-first-century churches still speak sixteenth-century English. Some pastors still wear paraphernalia from another century, another land, and another time. The original meaning is lost.

During the Reformation, many of God's great leaders wrote hymns in the language of the people—according to the tunes, tempo, and styles of the music of the day. Now many Protestants are petrified in practice, still using the same music many generations later, ignoring the principle involved in their creation in the first place.

The architecture of many church buildings reflects the style of another century and another continent. I remember a young woman whom I had encouraged to attend a church close to her home. She indicated that she wasn't attending that church anymore. She said she had tried it, but it just didn't seem like church. "They don't have pews, just folding chairs." Here was a person from an active Christian family who associated "church" with the externals.

This "stained-glass culture" confuses external style, and substance. The history of every segment of the Christian movement contains elements of culture and tradition. Not to be confused with theology, the portion of the tradition about which I'm speaking is practice. Are culture and tradition wrong? No, unless they become roadblocks to the gospel. Tradition can be helpful. In a constantly changing world, it is comforting to know that some things are not changing for the sake of change. But when practices become obsolete, lose their meaning, and fail to communicate the message of Jesus Christ in a relevant way, the cultural, historic practices move from expressing a stained-glass culture to being a stained-glass barrier. Many declining mainline denominations established for four generations or more face this problem.

Some will say that we just need to educate people to appreciate the music and church practices that are part of our tradition. Such cultural chauvinism represents a blind spot among those within the culture. It is also unbiblical to require nonspiritual changes for people to become Christians. For example, it is easy for us to recognize the inappropriateness of requiring people who speak Mandarin Chinese to learn English before they can become Christians. But it is much harder for us to recognize the roadblocks within our own cultural system.

How do you move a church forward when it is petrified and self-centered in practice? How does a church become sensitive, relevant, and progressive for the sake of the mission of the church?

1. *The actionary church develops a mentality that sees itself on the cutting edge* by studying and discussing what the apostle Paul meant when he said "I have become all things to all men so that by all possible means I might save some"

(1 Cor. 9:22), and by studying the meaning of the incarnation of Christ. What is the message of the incarnation for the church today?

2. *The actionary church realizes that there will always be people in the Christian movement who confuse theology and practice, tradition and mission.* They need help and challenges just as Jesus helped and challenged the first-century Pharisees. Even in the Pharisees' opposition to Jesus, he reached out to them and won some.

3. *The actionary church makes sure that change is not simply for change's sake.* It ties progressiveness to mission and ministry. It must be relevant for a purpose. Relevance in a multicultural society may require a variety of ministries and perhaps even a variety of languages.

4. *The actionary church helps people distinguish between what is theological, and therefore unchangeable, and what is external and temporary.* It reflects on the history of the church and discovers that God speaks other languages besides English, German, and even Latin; that church buildings have taken many forms throughout the centuries; that King David did not play the pipe organ; that no musical instrument is more or less sacred than any other; and that Christians in other cultures have used a great variety of styles of worship.

5. *The actionary church wrestles with these important questions:* What does it mean to be a member of your denomination? Is it a certain songbook? a certain style of worship? a certain language? certain foods? Or, is it what you believe and confess? These are the ways in which your church can determine when it should become progressive and when it is petrified.

Planned or Pasteurized?

Pasteurization is the process of heating a liquid to destroy objectionable organisms without altering the basic nature of the liquid. Pasteurized liquids are considered partially sterile.

Some people in the church look at the task of planning that way. They see it as a sterile, boring task. It should be just the opposite. Planning and goal setting are good stewardship tasks. Proverbs 13:16 says, "Sensible people always think before they act, but stupid people advertise their ignorance" (TEV).

To avoid planning, some people say that when we make plans and set goals, we are not placing the ministry in the hands of God, or that we are bringing secular methods into the work of God's kingdom. Those critics tend to think with an either-or mentality. Either you plan and set goals, or you let God do it. But the Scriptures have a both-and mentality. Proverbs 16:9 says, "In his heart a man plans his course, but the Lord determines his steps." Proverbs 16:1 says, "To man belong the plans of the heart, but from the Lord comes the reply of the tongue." The principle of Scripture is to make plans and to trust God. We should work as though we do it all and pray as if God does it all. Indeed, ministry is a partnership. God has decided to use people to build his kingdom. It is not one or the other. It's a partnership. It's both.

Planning simply says that what we do, we do "on purpose." Using our God-given intelligence and seeking God's direction, we make plans and set goals. Goals are like targets. They are important because without goals we cannot aim and we often don't even shoot. God has a grand plan to make disciples of all peoples. If we don't have plans, how can we say that we are in partnership in God's mission? We apply God's plan for all peoples to our plans for the people we can reach.

The decision-making board was gathered for its third monthly meeting since Pastor Smith arrived. Pastor Smith had been relatively quiet at previous meetings but felt like he'd earned the right to speak. With some hesitancy, Pastor Smith asked the group, "Do you ever set any goals?" Carl, a lifelong farmer from that area and oldest member of the elders, responded, "Set what?" With that short response, the pastor had the answer. The congregation had never intentionally set goals or developed plans or set strategies for reaching those goals. But what is interesting about Carl (and so many other Christians) is that at home he sets goals and makes plans all the time. As a successful farmer, he has had to set goals, develop strategies, and cautiously implement those strategies. He planned for the harvest.

When it comes to the Lord's harvest, most Christians don't set goals. Some Christians believe it's inappropriate. Occasionally those who feel that planning and goal setting undermine the sovereignty of God are preachers. They live out an interesting inconsistency. Every preacher agrees that the Holy Spirit is active when a message from God's Word is being preached. Every good preacher spends time studying and preparing (planning). The preparation doesn't undermine the work of the Holy Spirit. It often helps a lot. It's not an either-or, it's a both-and. It's a partnership.

How do you move your church to action in goal setting?

1. *Start asking these questions at every opportunity*: What is the role of this church in the mission of God? What is the plan for this year? What is the goal for ten years from now? Begin to help people start thinking about the future and how God wants the church to get there.

2. *Set aside time for the decision-making group in the church to go on an annual retreat away from the church lasting at least a couple of days*. The retreat should concentrate on fellowship, spiritual growth, planning, dreaming, and goal setting. The leaders of the church should declare their perception of God's will as they plan to work out the strategies with God's guidance and help.

3. *Graph your progress in various activities around the church*. Make growth projections for next year and the next five years. Develop strategy action plans for each area of projected growth. Use a tool like my book *Facing the Facts for*

Church Growth (Corunna, Ind.: Church Growth Center, 1982) to diagnose and plan for future health and growth.

4. *Work the plan.* The church moves to action because there is a direction to follow. This plan is not set in concrete and can always be changed. Work at it, review it, change it. But use it. Help the church to move forward intentionally.

5. *Help every family in the church develop a personal plan for discipleship.* This should be a part of parenting. It's the church's responsibility to help parents develop a family plan for discipleship growth.

6. *Develop a plan for outreach for your church to reach the different people groups in your community.* Plan the work. Work the plan.

Organized or Ossified?

"To ossify" means to become hard or rigid, to become bonelike. In the extreme, it can mean to become calloused and hardened. Many people think that when you organize the church, it will inevitably become ossified. But organization doesn't have to be that way. Organization in the church, done God's way, is alive, vital, and active.

The Christian church is supposed to be organized for action, not organized for order. One of the greatest teachings that came out of the Reformation was a reemphasis on the New Testament principle of the priesthood of all believers. Whenever the Christian movement has taken on vitality, it has recaptured this important grassroots notion.

Mobilizing the laity is a key to discipleship and mission in a healthy church. Actionary churches will emphasize the importance of people getting involved. The real key to mobilizing laypeople is helping them discover their spiritual gifts in the Body of Christ. This functional view of church membership affirms that every member has a gift. Every member has a function. Every member is important.

Everyone is a minister. This is God's plan to get the work of the church accomplished. God gives leaders to equip the people. When we organize the church the way God intended, it will be organized for action. It will be organized for ministry.

Many churches reflect the belief that ministry is the same thing as meetings. People meet and think that they are involved in some sort of ministry. Sometimes ministry does happen in meetings, but often meetings discourage more than encourage, tire more than inspire, and tear down more than build up. The key question to ask of any meeting is whether the activity is helping people grow in discipleship and move the church forward in mission. Most churches would be healthier and more active if they were not so busy with meetings. Focus on function. Every person in a congregation should be able to identify one or more ministries in which he or she is or can be involved.

People hear the word *organization* and think about details in the form of minutes, bylaws, policies, and procedures. Organization in the Christian church does call for details, but the details have to do with individuals. The church is person oriented rather than structure oriented. That's the way God intends the Body of Christ to be organized.

As churches get larger, they require different types of organization. Many large churches flounder because they are still organized like small churches. A large church is not simply a larger form of a smaller church. It's a different church. As a different church, it must have more formal communication and a different style of decision making.

Churches larger than two hundred in worship are sometimes struggling because they still follow informal communication patterns. Many decisions are made in the parking lot, over the backyard fence, or by means of the telephone. Small churches can operate that way. But in the large church, that's the way to make people angry. More formal communication is necessary.

For decision making in a large church, pure democracy in

which everybody decides everything is a stumbling block. Even in the small church this is impossible. Congregational meetings should only decide "the more important things." In the large church, the more important things are more numerous and more complicated. They demand much homework. They require sanctified common sense. Not everybody in the church has that. Consequently, larger congregations that are still operating as pure democracies have long congregational meetings filled with frustration.

Larger congregations are more appropriately organized like the form of government called a "republic." In a republic everybody chooses the leaders, and the leaders make the decisions. If they are good leaders, they will listen to their "constituents." Nevertheless, a few make the decisions for the many. If the many don't like the decisions of the few, they elect different leaders.

There is no biblical mandate for organizing a church in terms of a democracy or a republic. One is no more biblical than the other. But in larger churches the republic is simply more practical. How do you move your church to action?

1. *Get your people involved in studying spiritual gifts.* There are many books on the subject—including the Bible. Some students of spiritual gifts have developed questionnaires or surveys to help people identify their own gifts. These are not inspired biblical tools; they simply provide a way to stimulate people to think about spiritual gifts. Used for that purpose, they help the Christian to think about the functions of ministry in the variety of dimensions found in the New Testament church.

2. *Consider the way your church is organized.* Is it person centered, or is it structure centered? How is the church organized for service to people at the time of a funeral? How is it organized for families desiring growth and discipleship? How is it organized for ministry to people who are homebound? How is it organized for the newcomer or visitor to your church?

3. *Ask these questions:* Does the organization of the church fit present-day needs? Was the church organized many years ago in an era when the needs of the community were far different? Is there a need for change?

4. *Recognize that the constitution of your congregation is really not that important.* Some people get excited about changing the constitution. But the form of church structure that exists on paper does not automatically translate into action. Usually, the attitude of the people establishes the direction in which they function more than any form. I've seen congregations with outdated constitutions that simply find a creative way to work around their constitutions. Constitutions are made for one purpose: They are an objective guideline to follow when people get angry at one another and can no longer rationally deal with issues without their emotions getting in the way.

More important than a constitution is a philosophy of ministry statement or a mission statement for the church. This short, task-oriented statement tells about the uniqueness of the church and its mission at this important time in history. It is a document to share with potential new members and prospects and to use in advertising the uniqueness of the congregation to the community. Of course, a mission statement needs to be updated regularly and reviewed to ensure its relevance.

5. *Organize for discipleship.* If the goal of the Christian church is to make disciples, then it should be organized to do so. One way to discover whether your church has discipleship as a goal is to ask "What happens to new members of the congregation?" Are they led to a lifestyle of continual learning and growing in the Word, in stewardship, in witnessing, in prayer, and in other areas of the Christian life? The other question to ask is this: "Is the church organized for mission and outreach?" Are people learning to share their faith? Are Sunday school children encouraged to bring unchurched friends? Are home Bible study groups organized for outreach and not just for members? Can a

visitor who is not yet a member sing in the choir or play on the church basketball team? Does the first-time visitor feel welcomed by many people?

The answers to these questions will help you discover that moving the church to action is more than an organizing activity in the institutional sense. It calls for developing an attitude, a priority, a lifestyle, a worldview formed by the Lord's Word and the Holy Spirit. This attitude will determine your perception as a congregation of what business you are really in.

Discussion Questions

1. How do you measure the size of your church? Is this realistic? Is it God-pleasing? What actions can you take to bring a closer correspondence between the numbers shown on your membership rolls and the numbers who worship during a typical week?

2. Of the six areas of health discussed, how do you diagnose your church?

3. Of the six areas discussed, where are you strongest? Where are you weakest?

4. Is a risk-oriented church consistent with Jesus' commission to make disciples of all peoples? To what extent do sin, better judgment, stewardship, faith, zeal, and limitation of resources enter into your decisions?

5. Does failure of a plan, process, or program to attain its goal leave your church with nothing but a bad taste and negative feelings? What are the positive effects?

6. Are most, if not all, of your congregation's decisions based on an either-or assessment? List recent circumstances where both-and would have met the real needs of your people.

7. How does the organization of your congregation hinder or hamper its mission? Is it appropriate to the size of your church? How would you organize your church to move it most effectively into action?

3

WHAT BUSINESS ARE YOU IN?

One of the most important issues facing the church today is to clarify its purpose. Why does the church exist? What are its priorities? What has God called the church to be and to do?

The Scriptures say that the church is fighting against principalities and powers. In this great cosmic battle, Satan wants to destroy the church and plunder those who would be citizens of God's kingdom. But God has already won the victory in Jesus Christ. When Christ died on the cross, he beat Satan once and for all. Nevertheless, Satan continues to work to win people for his kingdom.

Satan's most insidious strategy is to attack the church not from the outside but from within. He aims to get Christians sidetracked on other issues and out of step with the primary purpose of the church. If he can sidetrack Christians, he renders their witness powerless and ineffective for extending God's kingdom. The millions who do not know Christ remain safe in Satan's realm because they do not know the gospel, and they will not hear it from an ineffective, sidetracked, and floundering church.

I often wonder how I went all the way through college, seminary, and graduate school (where I received a doctorate in theology) without asking "What is the main purpose of the church?" I was called to be a pastor of a congregation and still had never asked that question. I had been in a parish for several years before I even considered the question. I'm sure that I subconsciously had some ideas. Somewhere along the line it must have been discussed in one of my classes. But, as many of my classmates agree, it certainly wasn't emphasized. How did we get so far away from the basics?

There are five common issues that often sidetrack the church these day. Each issue describes important work for the church and good, Christian things to do. But none of them represents the main priority—the main purpose—of the church. However, for many churches, one of these issues becomes the main business.

1. *Helping the poor.* Today, as always, there is an abundance of poor people in the world. As Jesus said, "The poor you will always have with you, and you can help them any time you want" (Mark 14:7). Jesus often emphasized in both word and deed the need to care for those who are poor. Today, television brings into our living rooms the starving people of Ethiopia, the pain and sorrow reflected by the masses in the poverty of Calcutta, and the loneliness of the homeless in the war-torn areas of Central and South America and the Middle East. Ignoring these people would be a denial of the Christian faith. Nevertheless, to make service the main purpose of the church, the top priority for which God has called his people together, would ultimately leave these people without Jesus Christ, who is the Way, the Truth, and the Life, and who gives salvation now and for eternity.

2. *Social justice.* Some churches have entered the political arena to seek social justice for certain groups of people. Although such ecclesiastical politics may at times be an important Christian activity, it is not the priority for which God has called his people to be his church, nor the mission with which the Father charged his Son and his Son challenged his disciples. Indeed, it will often be an exercise in frustration for those who are seeking change through politics.

3. *Christian unity.* Many Christians today are working diligently on the priority of getting all Christians together in one church structure. Although this is an admirable goal, it is not the priority for the church. Our Lord certainly prayed for Christian unity. Indeed, all Christians share one faith, one hope, and one baptism. We share one Lord and Savior of us all. It is important to witness and give testimony to that unity in Christ whenever possible. But organizational unity is not a main priority for the church. It is not what the church has been called to do. Churches that spend the majority of their time, effort, and energy on issues of Christian unity are sidetracked from the main purpose for which God has called his church together.

4. *Faddism.* Sometimes churches jump from one fad to another. The pastor's sermon is likely to be heavily influenced by the headlines of recent newspapers. Although it is important for the church to meet the needs of people and to speak to the issues about which members are concerned, these needs are to be a bridge across which the gospel can reach people in a relevant way.

Recently, churches have been involved in discussions about homosexuals, abortion, AIDS, and futurism. These are all important topics, and the church must indeed say something about them and help those who need God's mercy and love in each situation. But the main purpose of the church is not to issue statements about homosexuality, change the world's thinking about abortion or AIDS, or be involved in futurism. Issues come and go, but the main purpose of the church is timeless; it remains the same until the Lord returns.

5. *Preserving tradition.* Some churches believe that their primary mission is to preserve historic tradition. Some church buildings have even been made into museums. But are they the church? Certainly not in the biblical sense. The church has not been called to preserve architecture, art, or tradition. Ultimately, there is nothing sacred about any

period of history, any tradition of architecture, art, music, or literature. The only thing that is sacred is the Word of God. It is fine—if it is culturally helpful—to preserve traditions, art, music, and architecture. It is good to emphasize the value of these things. But that is not the primary business of God's people.

Moreover, it is not even the primary business of the church to preserve traditions of religious language and theological classifications. The message of the church is the message of the Scriptures, which is the message of Jesus Christ, and that message is not to be compromised. But the form and traditional wording of the message is not a primary concern of the church.

In his ministry, Jesus was always intentional. When people tried to get him sidetracked, he would respond, "I must be about my Father's business" (Luke 2:49 KJV). He was clear about his mission and determined about his direction. Jesus told his disciples that there was no choice: He must turn his face toward Jerusalem. Not even the ugly event of the cross and the pain and suffering that it would mean would dissuade him. As he prayed in the Garden of Gethsemane, the Lord was clear about his mission. He said to his heavenly Father, "Not my will, but yours be done" (Luke 22:42). What was his purpose? What was his Father's business? What was his mission? To answer these questions, one has to ask "What was Jesus Christ doing on the cross?" and "What was the main purpose for which he died?"

Jesus Christ did not hang on the cross primarily to help the poor be relieved of their sorrow, pain, and hunger. He did not die to overcome the social injustices his people suffered at the hands of the Romans. He did not shed his blood for the ultimate purpose of visible Christian unity. (Jesus indicated that he would actually cause divisions— even in families.) He did not go to Calvary because of the popular fads of his day. He cleansed lepers, but he did not make healing his main theme. As the Pharisees could attest, he certainly wasn't on a mission of preserving tradition.

Jesus gave his life on the cross of Calvary so that sinful people on their way to death could have forgiveness and life. He took their place on that cross to reconcile the world—to make them one with God again. His concern was for the salvation of lost humanity. He extended his mission through his followers when he told them that if they forgave the sins of any, they would be forgiven, and if they would retain the sins of any, they would be retained. The primary purpose of God's mission in Jesus Christ and Christ's mission through his disciples is clearly the salvation of all people. In that mission, Jesus calls people today to repentance and gives them forgiveness through God's grace. He wants people to grow in that grace, to grow in fellowship, to reach out and share the message of forgiveness with others, and to multiply churches until his kingdom reaches the ends of the earth.

THE CASE OF THE U.S. RAILROADS

How important is it to know what business you are in? The United States railroads are a historic example. How different the world would be if the railroads had understood the business they were in. Unfortunately, most of the U.S. railroad companies thought they were in the railroad business. That was fine as long as there were no highways, automobiles, or airplanes. It was a great business to be in as long as the West was expanding and the best way to travel was by rail.

But today many of the U.S. railroads are almost out of business or highly subsidized. The reason? They failed to see their real business. The railroad companies were not in the railroad business. They were in the transportation business. Failure to realize this led to the demise of much of the railroad system in the United States.

Travel in the United States today would be quite different had the railroads defined their business as transportation. If they had, there would no doubt be transportation centers— large hubs of interconnected systems—in the United States today. Our whole world of travel would be different.

SEARS, ROEBUCK AND COMPANY

Being able to articulate clearly what business you are in is especially important when facing change. As management expert Peter Drucker notes in his book *Management: Tasks, Practices, Responsibilities* (New York: HarperCollins, 1974), this has been demonstrated in American enterprise throughout the history of Sears, Roebuck and Company.

What business is Sears in? Some people would say that it is catalog marketing, others would say retail sales. But the Sears people define their business as "service to people." Holding to that identity, that carefully defined business purpose, Sears has been able to withstand enormous change and to remain effective. Sears began during the years when the Wild West was being won. People were moving across the western plains of the United States and settling in areas where there were no stores or manufacturing outlets. With the growing delivery systems of the U.S. railroads and postal service, Sears saw an opportunity to sell goods to people through a catalog order system. But they did not define their business as catalog sales. If they had, they would just about be out of business today.

The next major trend in the United States that had an impact on Sears was the great influx of people into the industrial centers of the country. People flooded the cities seeking better-paying jobs in the factories. With the growth of urban areas came department stores. It was relatively easy for Sears to make the shift in the midst of that enormous change in demographics, primarily because they did not define their business as catalogs. Their business clearly articulated was "service to people." The people moved to the cities, so Sears began an emphasis in the cities. People began to shop at department stores, so Sears developed a network of department stores. But they did not define their business as department store sales. They were still in the business of "service to people." That was essential, especially when further major demographic changes took place in the United States.

As urban centers became overcrowded, the crime rate and the cost of living rose. The quality of urban life declined. The American people became wealthier and turned more and more to the automobile. People no longer rode in streetcars or buses in great numbers. Improved roads and highways were built, enabling people to move out of the cities and into suburbs. Shopping centers were developed in the new areas where the people lived, and these malls offered acres of extra parking. Since Sears had not defined its business as department store sales, it was now easy for the company to move with the people to the malls in the suburbs. After all, the company's business was "service to people."

Another major shift for Sears has not been a geographical change but a change in the world of business. The United States has been moving toward becoming an information society. The wide use of computers and information systems has produced a growing demand for information services. Sears added financial, real estate, and insurance services to its retail business. This may seem odd to the casual shopper who thinks that Sears is in the business of selling retail goods. But when one recognizes that the clearly articulated business of Sears is "service to people," it all makes sense.

Most recently Sears reduced prices, reflecting once again sensitivity to the people the company serves and flexibility to adapt to a changing world. Sears is able to remain viable because the company is clear about its mission.

What does this have to do with the church? The church is in the midst of constant change. The church must never change its message, but in form, style, communication technique, and delivery systems the church must change if it is to remain a relevant and powerful force in the world.

Some churches are like the railroads. They are in disrepair, depend on large subsidies, and reflect a past era. Other churches are alive, healthy, and vibrant. They have changed with the times and have adapted in ways that make the unchanging gospel meaningful to their changing world.

The key is understanding your purpose. If the church defines its purpose as maintaining tradition—speaking the language of the old country, preserving the architecture from a certain era, and perpetuating what have become meaningless patterns—it becomes an irrelevant curiosity for those who are not part of the tradition. At the other extreme, if the church jumps at every fad and notion that is popular, it becomes meaningless and powerless. The church plays politics but can't really play the game as well as the experts. The church gets involved in social programs but really doesn't have the depth and resources to match what government programs can offer. Consequently, the church is often playing to its weaknesses rather than to its strengths.

Asking what business your church is in means also asking what the church can do most effectively. What can the church offer that no one else can offer? What is the priority and the mission of the church, according to God? Why did Jesus die on the cross? What was he doing on this earth? What was he doing at Calvary? What did he gather his disciples together to do? What is the mission? What is the Great Commission?

First Church is a good example of a congregation that, like the railroads, wasn't clear about what business it was in. First Church is located in an urban neighborhood. During the late 1940s and early 1950s, the church grew dramatically, as many people from the denomination moved into the community and transferred their memberships to the church. They brought with them many of their friends, relatives, and neighbors who were unchurched.

There was much excellent ministry at First Church. But somehow the clearly articulated business of the church got lost in the busyness and activities of the "ministry." There were basketball teams, baseball teams, and musicals. The congregation hosted roller-skating parties, picnics, and many fellowship suppers. The church even owned its own park. Bowling became popular, and the congregation built several bowling lanes in the basement of the educational wing.

What was the clearly articulated business of First Church? There really wasn't any. Busyness and activity seemed to be the trademark of the church. Was the church in the business of bowling, basketball, roller skating, or fellowship suppers? Not really, but sort of. First Church seemed to be an exciting place. It probably never occurred to anybody that it was important to remember the identity and uniqueness of what it means to be the church and to be "about the Father's business."

Then something happened that no one foresaw. The neighborhood began to change. The Anglos began to move out, and the Hispanics began to move in. The Anglos and the Hispanics did not speak the same language. They did not eat the same foods. They did not live the same lifestyles. They did not share the same economic levels. Consequently, they did not associate with each other much. Therefore there was little outreach through basketball, bowling, picnics, and fellowship suppers.

First Church began to decline in membership. As the members got older, there were many more funerals. The children of the members who grew up in distant suburbs were not as loyal to the building and the ministry. They began to visit churches in their own communities where they could see their peers from school. Finally, the number of Anglos who would drive down to the old neighborhood to attend "their" church became so small that they could no longer heat the aging building or pay the insurance. First Church could not handle the change because the members were unclear about what business they were in.

In an almost identical setting in a different metropolitan area, a church like First Church went through the same changes at about the same time. But Redeemer Church had one key difference. The pastors and the key leaders had carefully articulated that the main purpose of the church was to make disciples and to be in mission to all people everywhere. The church approached its Hispanic community as an opportunity for ministry and outreach. They called a Spanish-speaking pastor and began to meet the needs in the community. The transition was hard, but there was a strong continuity reflected in clarity of purpose. This provided the church with a clear mission and resulted in a healthy and vibrant Christian church.

YOUR BUSINESS SHAPES YOUR ACTION

Knowing what business you are in shapes everything you do. If your church believes that helping the poor is the primary purpose of the church, that will shape its priorities. As you consider the business of your church, what do its priorities reflect? What is most important to the pastor? What is most important to the leaders? Where is the time, energy, and money spent? Do members talk about the main purpose of the church? Is it discussed in Bible classes? Is it presented to youth groups? Is it taught in Sunday school? Do you hear it in sermons? Does the average person in your church know what business the church is in according to what God says in his Word? If you conducted a survey among people in your church concerning its main purpose, what would you discover?

The fundamental issue concerns individual attitudes and worldviews. A worldview is the way you see yourself, your church, your community, and your world. Do you see yourself as an ambassador of Christ, a missionary, or a witness? Do the people of your church see themselves as called to be disciples and to make disciples? As Darrow L. Miller points out in *Discipling Nations* (Seattle: YWAM Publishing, 1998), worldview determines behavior; ideas have consequences.

The attitudes and worldviews of the members will shape the programming of the church. What we do in life does not shape how we think. It works the other way around. How we think determines how we act. Paul Yonggi Cho, pastor of the largest church in the world in Seoul, South Korea, said it this way during a 1992 church growth conference: "Sometimes we believe that we shape our dreams. But we really don't. They shape us."

Programming reflects our thinking and our attitudes. Programs and activities are secondary. One of the frustrations for many churches today is that most resources are produced to be used at the program level of the church. But that often serves only to get at symptoms rather than at the root of the problem—the attitudes and worldviews of the people. The church can purchase the greatest evangelism program in the world from the fastest-growing church in the history of Christianity, but if you invite people to come out to evangelism training using this program, the number of people who will ignore the invitation is not directly proportional to the value of the program. It is directly proportional to the attitudes of the people toward evangelism. Nevertheless, most of the resources that come from denominations, Christian agencies, and publishing companies are program oriented. Why? Because that's what church leaders want. They are looking for a quick fix for the church. But the church needs more.

We live in a microwave world—a world of instantaneous results. People expect immediate results and immediate change. People want to run programs, not cultivate other people. Yet isn't cultivation precisely what Jesus did? In the last three years of his life—his entire earthly ministry—he spent most of his time with just a few people. Day and night he lived with his disciples. He modeled ministry, taught them, opened up his life to them, and inspired and motivated them as he cultivated them. He sent them out, brought them back to debrief, and sent them out again. On the day of Pentecost he empowered them just as he had promised, and they were released to carry on his ministry.

Many churches today want to run programs rather than develop people. Actionary churches have leaders who see the need for getting back to the basics—to develop people's attitudes and worldviews.

During the last several years, I have been part of a team of creative people who have designed a process aimed at developing an attitudinal change within a congregation over a period of several years. Through a series of learning events and experiences, monitoring, and directed help from the outside, this process provides a comprehensive approach for the intentional change of worldviews.

Nearly five hundred churches in several regions of the United States and Canada and from several denominations have participated in this process. Some of the results have been phenomenal. Christians are growing in discipleship. Churches that were declining or plateaued are growing. Facilities are being built. Churches are being planted. Members are discovering their spiritual gifts. Churches are working and planning for the mission of the church. This demonstrates that one of the keys to moving your church into action is to deal with attitudes and worldviews. It is clearly a matter of defining what business you are in—not simply as a corporate body called the church, but as the individual people who are the church. The key ingredients of this change are that (1) it is a process; (2) it is comprehensive; (3) it requires patience, directing the church over a long period of time; and (4) it deals with attitudes as the primary focus.

◆

Roadblock People

People who want to move the church into action will run into roadblock people. Generally speaking, there are two kinds of roadblock people.

I introduce to you Alan Ignorant and Abigail Apathetic. Al and Abi are representative of many church members. They are nice people. They are your friends. They love the Lord and appreciate their church. They are secure in their trust in Jesus Christ alone for salvation. Like you, they share in the solid hope of the resurrection to eternal life.

But they are different. They don't look different, and for the most part they don't act different. But a piece of their makeup is missing. Somehow they missed the vision of what the church is to do and to be. They never clearly grasped the main purpose of the church. They missed the mission.

Alan Ignorant and Abigail Apathetic have much in common. They both unintentionally inhibit your church from moving to action. But there are some differences between Al and Abi. These differences help determine the proper strategies for reaching each of them. What are the differences? That is best explained through an experience that one of their friends, Sam, had at school just the other day.

Sam was sitting at the back of the classroom half asleep when the teacher asked the class, "What is the difference between ignorance and apathy?" No one answered. The teacher, noticing that Sam was dozing off in the back row, jolted him awake with the direct question: "Sam, what is the difference between ignorance and apathy?"

Sam was a bit startled. After a poorly concealed yawn, he said, "I don't know ... and I don't care."

"You're right!"

The ignorant are those who say, "I don't know." The apathetic are those who say, "I don't care." Both attitudes are roadblocks to moving the church into action. Each of them requires a different strategy.

The "I don't know" people, led by Alan Ignorant, simply need to be taught what business the church is in. They can attend a workshop, see a film, take part in a Bible class, listen to a set of audiotapes, or read a book on the primary purpose of the church. If they are invited in a winsome way, chances are they will participate in one of these activities and move from the realm of ignorance to a clearer understanding of what God has called the church to do and to be. They will come to realize the importance of the discipleship lifestyle. They will begin to see themselves as part of the mission to which God has called his people—to reach out with the good news to the ends of the earth.

Abigail Apathetic is representative of a much larger group than Alan's, unfortunately. They present a greater challenge for change. By "apathetic" I mean those who attend church regularly but never sing in the choir, never attend Bible class or Sunday school, do not serve in leadership positions, and do not get involved in activities. They are too busy, too tired, too involved in other things. For them, "it's just not the right time"—ever! Of course, there are occasions when members can be too busy or too involved in other things. There are times when it is legitimately the wrong time. But for genuinely apathetic people, this is a consistent pattern.

The strategy for reaching the apathetic is complex. Apathetic people ultimately must move from apathy to ignorance. At that point, the first strategy noted above is applied. But how are they moved from apathy to ignorance? The strategy for reaching apathetic people is based on two premises. Premise 1: In order for apathetic people to want to change, you must first raise their level of discontent. The second premise: The only way Christians can ethically raise the level of discontent in other Christians is by the application of Scripture. The biblical message of Law and gospel will enable them to see their sins and their failures, their need for a Savior, their need for a change. It will enable them to find joy in their Savior's love, and forgiveness, as well as the power to live, change, and serve.

Combining these two premises for reaching apathetic people with the biblical and social principle of web relationships, which says that every person has a small group of "significant others" who have influence over them, I have developed an Apathy Buster Strategy. Here's how it works: Begin with prayer. Ask the Lord to guide and direct you in this important project. Then carefully invite fifteen to twenty active people who are neither ignorant nor apathetic to your home for an evening of food, fellowship, and Bible study. Approach each individually. Make no major announcements to the congregation. This is not a big program; it's a process.

In the social setting of your home, introduce a Bible study on the nature of the church. Use an inductive Bible study in which the group does the Bible study by itself. You as leader simply call the group together and make sure that it is loosely organized and eventually gets to the task of the Bible study. Other than that, the leader does not dominate. This is inductive leadership. One such study that many churches have used is my book *Six Faces of the Christian Church: How to Light a Fire in a Lukewarm Church* (Corunna, Ind.: Church Growth Center, 1983). This tool is designed to raise discontent.

During this first Bible study, model the inductive leadership style to the group. Do not dominate. Do not put anyone on the spot. Simply take turns reading the material. Let the group members answer the questions as a group, with individuals responding as they wish. At the end of the study, ask the members if they would like to do it again.

Was it fun? Would they like to get together again and move on to chapter 2 of the study? Most will usually agree to do so. Pick a date, time, and place that is most convenient. Choose a method of supplying food or refreshment that is most suitable to the group.

On the last evening of the study (perhaps after six to eight months), ask those present if they would like to do the same thing that you have done, inviting their friends in the congregation who are not presently involved in a home Bible study group. Some of the potential leaders will agree to do this, while others may decline. Share a membership list of the congregation with those who agree. Let each leader choose people with whom he or she already feels comfortable. Ask each to choose fifteen to twenty people, approximately one-third of whom are not involved in any activities but who attend church regularly (the apathetic).

As you look at the membership list, go around the room and let the leaders have first choices. Then go around the room again and let them have second choices. Do this until they run out of people with whom they feel comfortable, or until they each reach a total of no more than twenty people.

These leaders will then follow the same strategy. They will begin in prayer. They will invite people individually into their homes for food, fellowship, and Bible study for one evening only. At the end of the evening, they will extend a further invitation to those who want to continue with the Bible study.

Since two-thirds of the group is made up of nonapathetic people, and since they are "significant others" of the apathetic third, exciting dynamics will take place. As the Bible study is used, the Scriptures will challenge the entire group to reflect on the nature of the church. As they do, the nonapathetic people will naturally give testimony in front of their apathetic peers. Those who are apathetic will be challenged by the Scriptures, and they will be enlightened by the Spirit-directed attitudes and worldviews expressed by their spiritually mature peers.

In the noninstitutional, friendly setting of the home—reinforced by social bonds and fellowship—the scriptural description of the nature of the church, and the biblical understanding of what God has called the church to be and to do will simmer gently in the hearts and minds of those who are apathetic. The Spirit, who gives God's Word power, will, over a period of lessons, raise their level of discontent, kindle their desire for spiritual change, and move the apathetic people toward the realm of activity, thereby removing them as roadblock people and developing them into people who want to move to action.

IDENTITY CRISIS IN THE CHURCH

If the church wants to move to action, it must know what business it is in. The roadblock people must be renewed by God's Spirit through the study of the Word. As a growing number of people in the church come to see what the church is and what it is to do, God will move the church to action. An increased awareness of the nature of Christ's body—the church—will mean a new understanding for many who were raised in the church and who subtly came to believe that the church is an institution. Seeing the church as an organism in whom Christ lives will open up new horizons for the congregation that is coming alive and moving to action.

Discussion Questions

1. How do you feel about comparing your church to a business? In a few words, what do you believe is the real reason for which your church exists?

2. Consider the five issues offered as the main business of the church. Are any of them detractors or irrelevant to the spreading of the gospel? How many might be considered by-products rather than the main purpose?

3. Is it ungodly to use the examples of business success and the knowledge gleaned from proven technology and social and applied sciences as models for church behavior? When might such applications be inappropriate?

4. What categories of roadblock people do you have in your church? Develop a strategy to overcome each of them.

5. What would it cost (in every way) to initiate the Apathy Buster Strategy in your congregation? Would the rewards be worth the time, costs, and risks? Will you try it?

4

INSTITUTION OR ORGANISM?

Pastor Bronnstein sat in the third row of the seminar room, anxiously awaiting the beginning of the training event. He was surprised and elated when his classmate, Pastor Schaefer, entered the room. They had not seen each other since seminary and had served congregations in different states. Both had flown to Philadelphia to attend a training event on how to get laypeople involved in visiting nursing homes. After the seminar, both returned to their respective congregations to implement the valuable principles they had learned.

Pastor Bronnstein decided to share as much as possible from the seminar with his people at Zion Church. He wrote an article for the church newsletter explaining the importance of nursing-home ministry. Then he planned a number of classes on the subject and publicized them in the church bulletin for several weeks. The publicity was supported by several verbal announcements on Sunday mornings. The five two-hour sessions were a great success. Nine people registered, and an average attendance of seven was recorded. Six of the nine people completed most of the homework that Pastor Bronnstein assigned. Most of them did quite well on the quiz that he gave the class. One year later, three people from the class were still involved in a nursing-home ministry on a regular basis.

Pastor Schaefer approached his congregation with a different strategy. He prayed, meditated, and reflected on the seminar he had attended. He asked God to guide him as he sought to share the principles of the nursing-home ministry with the people of Peace Church. He put a notice in the bulletin thanking the congregation for providing his trip to Philadelphia and for paying the tuition for the seminar. He asked the congregation to remember him in prayer as he sought ways to implement what he had learned.

The next week Pastor Schaefer went through the congregation's membership list. "We need for this ministry," he thought, "people who have the gifts of mercy or service or both."

Pastor Schaefer selected seven people who were either listed as having these gifts or appeared to have them because of ministries in which they had been involved. He knew that four of the seven people were not presently involved in a ministry. The next week he visited each of the four people in their homes. He asked them how things in general were going, how they felt about their Christian faith and life, and what their involvement in ministry was at that time. He shared with them his concern that no church had a formal ministry at two of the nursing homes in their area of the city. He asked them if they had ever known or visited anyone in a nursing home. Then he asked each one to pray about the possibility of accompanying him as a silent partner on a few visits to nursing homes. He closed each visit with prayer.

After a couple of weeks, he met with each person again. He asked them about their prayers after his previous visit. One of the members said it was a good idea and wanted to be involved but felt that it was a bad time because of pressures at work. The other three said they would gladly go along on a visit as long as they didn't have to say or do anything. Over the next six months, the pastor took each of the three with him on seven to ten visits. During the first five visits, the members were silent. After that, on the way to the nursing home the pastor asked them if they would like to participate. He would say, "Joe, you've seen me minister to a number of people during the last several visits. Would you like to say something or do something? Would you like to read the Scripture or have the prayer or do both?"

During the next several visits, each of the three began to get involved at his or her own pace. As each one gained confidence, the pastor suggested that if they split up at the nursing home, they could minister to twice as many people in the same amount of time. After the calls, they would stop for coffee and discuss what had happened.

During the three-month period that followed, the pastor became confident that these people were gifted in this area and felt called to such a ministry. He asked each of them if they would like to adopt it as a formal ministry until the Lord called them to do something else. Two of the three agreed that this was what the Lord was calling them to do. The third wanted to continue visiting with Pastor Schaefer.

At a morning worship service, Pastor Schaefer commissioned the two members who were ready to be nursing-home visitors. During the week after the commissioning service, the pastor shared with both members his hope and prayer that they would follow the same steps that he did. Beginning with prayer, he asked if they would seek out one or two more people who might be gifted for nursing-home ministry. They agreed to do so, and he pledged his support, encouragement, and cooperation.

At the end of one year, there were two commissioned nursing-home visitors. One was beginning to train three other members, and the other was beginning to train one other member.

The difference in these approaches reflects an institutional versus an organismic view of the church.

INSTITUTIONAL OR ORGANISMIC?

There are two ways churches function. The "institutional approach" is by far the most popular in many societies today. Institutionalism is one of the earmarks of a church that has moved from being a fledgling mission to a sophisticated entity. It doesn't have to happen that way, but it just usually does.

The other way a church functions is called the "organismic approach." The institutional approach tends to see functions within the church as programs; the organismic, or relational, understanding of the church is more likely to view Christianity as a movement. The institutional view of church life is more concerned with membership, titles, guidelines, bylaws, and regulations; it reflects a formalistic approach. The relational view of the church places more emphasis on worship attendance, activity, fellowship, ministries, personal Bible study, and individual personal testimony.

Those who view the church institutionally tend to see it in a one-dimensional way. They view the congregation much as a person looking at a photograph. They have an overview of the congregation that requires several generalizations about the church. Those who look at the church relationally see it as having multidimensional complexity, much like the human body. Rather than looking at the church as one views a photograph, they are more likely to see the church with the depth of a CAT scan, recognizing the various systems working within what is called the Body of Christ.

Institutional thinking about the church is so prevalent because in the last several centuries many people, especially in the Western world, have had a literal view of life. This is partly due to the emergence of the printing press, math, and the sciences. Literalists see things in either-or categories and tend to put everything in its place systematically. The institutional view of the church comes more naturally to them.

Other people are more conceptual by nature. They often think in both-and categories and tend to see the church as multidimensional and fluid. During Jesus' time, people were generally more conceptually oriented. So Jesus often communicated with parables and used object lessons like the lilies of the field. It should be no surprise that the Scriptures describe the church in conceptual imagery.

Throughout the Middle Ages, many people remained illiterate. Consequently, most of the great cathedrals in Europe, which date back to that period of history, are filled with stained-glass windows that conceptualize the stories of the Bible.

An interesting phenomenon is taking place today as the church moves to the age of action. More and more people are conceptually oriented. Some believe that this phenomenon is occurring because many people are being raised with television. The multimedia experience, it is conjectured, helps people to think in multidimensional ways. If more people are seeing the church conceptually, a far different worldview could develop in the church that will affect much of what takes place functionally within the local congregation.

THE CHURCH ALIVE

In the New Testament, there is no specific treatise that spells out all the details of what the church should be like. That's why there are so many different forms of church polity today.

There is no biblical—or "right"—way of carrying out many of the formal activities of a church. For example, the Bible doesn't specify at what times to schedule church services. It doesn't give blueprints on how to build a church building (unless you want to build a temple). It doesn't give guidelines on how to be a Sunday school teacher.

Instead, the New Testament gives a strong conceptual picture of the nature of the church, leaving the details of each individual church for the Spirit-led disciples to figure out. The New Testament uses several images to provide a framework for understanding the church, which is called the bride of the Bridegroom, Jesus Christ. It is called the sheep of the Good Shepherd, who is Jesus. Jesus says his people are the branches and he is the Vine. The New Testament calls God's people a royal priesthood, a holy nation. The church is a living temple of living stones, with Jesus Christ as the Chief Cornerstone, and the apostles and prophets as the foundation—a living temple that is a habitation for the living God. The people of God are called citizens of the Kingdom and ambassadors for their King, the Lord Jesus Christ. The people of God are called a family, and fellow members of the faith are brothers and sisters. Together we inherit God's promises. The church is called the Body of Christ, of which he is the Head. When each part works as it should, "the body grows and builds itself up in love" (Eph. 4:16).

These images have some common characteristics. The first is that God brings the church together. It is God's initiative. Second, Jesus Christ is in charge. His power and presence make the church the church. Third, the church itself is a living organism. Every one of these images is alive. Conceptually, the church is dynamic, fluid, living, moving, growing, and active. If you want to move your church to action, you're in good company because the Bible has an action bias about the church. This makes sense. A church can't be on a mission unless there is action.

As a church shifts in emphasis from being a movement to becoming an institution, it takes on certain characteristics:

1. *The church becomes more maintenance-centered and loses its action bias.* There is more interest in preserving, protecting,

and controlling than in accomplishing, conquering, and growing.

2. *Ministries that are fluid and often informal, based on gifts and tied directly to individuals who feel called to serve in them, are replaced by formal board and committee policy-making groups.* They don't do much ministry. Instead, they become centers of control and power, sometimes even to the extent that professional church workers must appear before this volunteer group of ecclesiastical amateurs to get permission to do their jobs. This is not to say that the board members are uncommitted Christians or that they lack wisdom or integrity. But they often mistakenly equate board and committee meetings with ministry. They usually meet at church after a long day at work when they are physically and mentally at their worst. They spend precious time separated from their families, meet in some pretty dingy environments, find themselves arguing vehemently with their fellow Christians, and return home late at night upset and unable to sleep for several hours. Yet they do feel some satisfaction because they believe that they have "served the Lord."

3. *The work of ministry revolves around the professionals.* Since the ecclesiastical amateurs have taken the leadership role, the person called to be the leader and equipper often takes the ministry role. Ministry is often centered around the pastor rather than the laity.

Michael Green, a historian of evangelism in the early church, has noted that Christianity was a lay movement in the New Testament. This was one of the reasons that the church grew so rapidly in its early years. That makes sense, since seventy-five laypeople can accomplish much more ministry in their spare time than one professional person can working full time. It makes even more sense when one understands that no individual, including a pastor, has all the spiritual gifts that make up the Body of Christ. It takes all the parts of the Body of Christ to do the ministry for which it was designed.

4. *The institutional form of the church, although not denying that Jesus Christ is the Head of his Body, the Vine of the branches, and the Bridegroom of the bride, tends to emphasize a board, a council, the elders, the deacons, a vestry, a session, and in some cases, the senior minister as the practical heads of the church.*

The church that is institutionally oriented is more apt to be involved in votes, debates, presentations, and arguments. Churches that reflect Christianity as a movement are more apt to pray, wait on the Lord, and simply not move on a project until the Lord brings about consensus among the sanctified leadership.

Many people say that congregational meetings at which everyone gets an opportunity to speak and to vote are the spiritual low point of the church's life. To comment that congregational meetings are often unproductive is an understatement. Some church leaders report that they have experienced congregational meetings that resemble events such as the Battle of the Bulge, the atomic bomb dropped on Hiroshima, or the gunfight at the O.K. Corral. There are basic reasons why some congregational meetings would fall outside the realm of acceptable Christian behavior.

First, when large groups come together to vote, there is often a tense atmosphere. If large groups convene simply to discuss, there is an entirely different environment. The pressure that accompanies decision making often prevents creative thinking about the issue in question.

Second, large-group decision making always leans toward the status quo. Pioneering, risk-oriented decisions are usually made by smaller groups, not larger groups.

Third, everyone in the congregation is invited to a congregational meeting and permitted to speak and to vote. This system gives unqualified people an opportunity to speak. Congregations give them the right to speak because they have joined the church. But that does not necessarily qualify them to guide the church's mission. They may not have done their homework, especially to the extent that the leaders have discussed, studied, and prayed about the issues. Further, they may not be spiritually qualified to speak publicly in the church decision-making process.

What are the results of congregational meetings like this? Three things generally happen, none of which is the stated purpose for such events.

1. *The leaders of the church often become discouraged.* They work hard, sacrifice much, and bring proposals to the church, only to have those who have not done their homework, or those who are spiritually immature, shoot down their ideas. These leaders are volunteers. They mean well. They are doing the best they can. But when they are publicly ridiculed or see their efforts and plans go up in smoke because of the comments of someone who perhaps doesn't even consider the mission for which the church exists, they become discouraged. It should surprise no one that congregations have difficulty finding volunteer leaders under these circumstances.

2. *Pastors tend to become discouraged and take calls to other churches.* It tears at the guts of a shepherd who loves his/her flock to see the flock embroiled in an emotional battle over what is so often a petty issue in the congregation's life. It destroys a pastor's enthusiasm to see the plans and efforts of months of work and preparation, based on years of education and experience, shot full of holes by a handful of people who do not like the music chosen for worship services. It wrenches the life out of a pastor to listen to a pompous member speak as if he were the sole contributor to the congregation, while the pastor knows full well that many of the Sunday school children give more to the work of the Lord annually than that member does.

3. *New members are subjected to the stresses of congregational meetings.* Some of these new members are baby Christians. Baby Christians, like babies in general, need protection from the stresses and strains of life until they mature.

Wise parents intentionally choose the time and the place

to have a heated discussion or to express disagreement. For example, they do not share their frustrations with each other over financial problems in front of the six- and seven-year-old children. It's not that they want to hide reality from their children; they simply understand that the children are not yet ready to deal with financial frustrations. Parents protect them. But in the Christian church family we often expose spiritual babies to the tensions and pressures of decision making that should be reserved for the spiritually mature.

The congregational meetings as the basis for all decision making is perhaps the greatest symbol of the institutional and organizational understanding of the church. As you seek to move your congregation into the age of action, ask yourself if the meetings edify those who are in attendance. Is the fruit of the Spirit evident?

THE "DOCTRINE" OF ELECTIONS

Some believe that electing all leaders by popular vote is a biblical teaching. It is not! It is more a reflection of a cultural setting of a church than a biblical mandate.

When leadership roles are filled by popular vote, the leaders may not be spiritually mature enough or spiritually gifted for the position. Often they are not trained for the position. Sometimes the position is not even carefully explained to the person.

The biblical way of fitting people into ministry areas is the discipleship model. It is not institutional; it is relational. Jesus discipled the Twelve. Paul discipled Timothy. Not only should every Christian be a disciple as a matter of lifestyle, but every disciple also should be discipling someone else.

As people are discipled, they grow in their maturity in Christ and in their understanding of the Bible. They learn about stewardship. They grow in their ability to witness to others of the hope within them. They begin to discover their spiritual gifts. As they discover their gifts, they recognize that they have a place in the ministry of the Body of Christ and seek ministries according to what God has intended them to do.

Churches that follow this biblical discipleship method often do not elect people to positions (the institutional way of doing things) but commission them to ministries. If the larger group wants control, a good system is to have the group ratify the commissioning of the individual for a ministry.

One of the institutional aspects that undermines the health and vitality of the church is annual elections. Ministries do not change with the calendar. They continue. If the pastor and leaders of the church are equipping the saints for ministry as Ephesians 4 directs, by the time a person has grown into a ministry, the church elects someone else. The system of annual elections all but guarantees that equipping and training for positions will be rendered ineffective.

People should be regarded as called to a particular ministry until God calls them to another ministry. This is the way most Sunday school positions are handled, but other positions in the church often do not follow this pattern.

How did all this get started? It is the influence of society. Churches are corporations. Corporations are required to have elections. The Bible says that the church is supposed to salt—that is, flavor—the world, but in this case the world has flavored the church. The travesty of this arrangement is that most Christians have not realized what this has done to the relational, organismic nature of the church. (Of course, congregations can improve the election process by developing guidelines and a selection process for the nominating committee to follow that is along the lines of biblical discipleship.)

What about new members? If people remain in positions for a long period of time, does that mean that the door is closed to new members? No, because every healthy and growing church should be constantly adding new ministries. As these new ministries develop, God will supply all of the needs of the congregation for all the challenges God places before it.

PROFESSIONAL CHURCH WORKERS

Even the training of professional church workers is patterned by an institutional bias. For example, little attention is paid to spiritual-gift analysis and discovery. The emphasis is strongly on academics in the context of a formal classroom. There is usually a period of internship for most pastors and other church workers. But this is a minimal amount of time in comparison to the formal institutional training.

One of the challenges facing denominations today is that church workers are not learning primarily by modeling. Some seminaries tend not to train parish pastors but instead do a good job of training seminary professors. Seminary professors are often academicians, not practitioners. Consequently, those who study under them learn by modeling how to be academicians, not practitioners.

Since pastors and other professional church workers learn how to be church workers in an institutional setting, one can see the challenge before the church to rethink the foundational model and structure for ministry as it moves into an age of action. What if every student wanting to be a pastor were required to serve an apprentice for several years before attending school?

Most people today have inherited an understanding of church that has an institutional bias. Granted, organization for mission is necessary. The Scripture describes the church as an ordered and orderly entity. But the less emphasis on institutionalism and the more that is placed on the church as an organism, the more likely the church is to move to action. God uses the Body of Christ as a powerful force. For Christianity to move into the age of action, the local church must break loose from bureaucracy and become a movement once again. If that is going to happen, an important ingredient will be leadership.

Discussion Questions

1. How do you view your church? Does it more closely resemble a worldly enterprise or a living creature? How is this evident?

2. Discuss the terms "institution" and "organism" with respect to their usage in this chapter. Which best describes you and your church?

3. List the practices or traditions in your church that are held to as if biblically commanded, but in reality are matters of minor spiritual significance.

4. How many images of the church are presented in the section "The Church Alive"? Which of these has the most appeal to you? Why?

5. Analyze your congregational meetings as to effectiveness and productivity, considering:

Who may participate?

Who may speak?

Who may vote?

Who demonstrates the best "homework"?

Who makes the most noise?

Who leads?

Who prevails?

Without being judgmental, consider which of these persons or groups edify and which debilitate the Body of Christ.

6. How are the officers and leaders of your church called,

elected, or chosen? Is there a better way? Evaluate your answer in terms of spiritual gifts, duration of term, experience, continuity of ministry, politics, spiritual maturity, biblical example, and family life.

7. (For professional church workers only) Knowing what you now know, if you had the opportunity to plan your education again, what omitted training would you desire? What could be de-emphasized or even omitted without jeopardizing your professional competence?

5

LEADERSHIP

One of the key ingredients in the mix for moving a church to action is leadership. In this chapter the subject will be dealt with in general and will be applied particularly to lay leadership in the church. In the next chapter the subject of the pastor as leader will be considered.

Leaders do lead. Sometimes, because of a false humility that has nothing to do with the gospel, Christians are hesitant to lead, especially to lead with vigor. When God calls leaders, he expects them to lead. The notion of leadership in the Scriptures suggests those who are out front leading the way. The New Testament identifies a spiritual gift of leadership (Rom. 12:8). This is a special attribute that the Spirit gives to certain members of the Body of Christ to inspire, motivate, and direct others who recognize their leadership and follow. Of course, many Christians who may not have the spiritual gift of leadership still exercise the role of a leader—as a Sunday school teacher, a member of a task force, or a Christian parent.

Christian leadership is a delegated responsibility from God. Those who lead are accountable ultimately to God himself (Heb. 13:17). Leaders move people toward goals, setting the direction and the pace for the church's gospel ministry. That's why they are so important as a church moves into the age of action.

Whenever God wants to accomplish something, he chooses a leader. The Old Testament is filled with examples in which God chose a particular person to move his plan of salvation forward. In the New Testament, God continued to use special people to do extraordinary tasks. God clearly understands that any group of people needs a leader. Every congregation needs the office of the public ministry. That leader is someone whom God has called for a specific and unique purpose.

CAUGHT, NOT TAUGHT

A person can read about the mechanics of leadership in a textbook, take courses in it, study styles of it, and even be elected to a position of leadership. Yet an elusive aspect of leadership is that some people actually lead and some do not. God gives his gift of leadership to whom he will. But even those who are gifted do not learn it academically. It is caught, not taught. This underscores the importance of modeling. God uses those who exhibit good leadership to train others to be leaders. This has seven implications for leadership in the Christian church.

1. *The time the pastor spends with lay leaders is essential.* Spending quality time with them empowers and equips them as leaders. In this way, the pastor is multiplied and increases the amount of Christian service that the congregation can perform among its members and for others. But this is not an academic exercise or simply a training in technique. It is a process of modeling character, commitment, attitude, worldview, and enthusiasm for Christ and his church. This assumes, of course, that the pastor personally reflects these positive attributes. If a church wants to move to action, the pastor should invest many hours with key laypeople in fellowship, Bible study, prayer, recreation, formal and informal discussion about the church, and ministry to people. The pastor is to be an active example (1 Pet. 5:3).

2. *Every leader should be discipling other leaders.* The task of

multiplication does not end with a pastor, but continues with every lay leader as well; leaders should always be working themselves out of a job. In a real sense, every Christian congregation is only one generation away from being without leadership. Since leadership can't simply be elected or taught, the current leaders need to find potential leaders and prepare them for the work that God has called them to do in the next generation.

Leighton Ford, moved by the death of his son, Sandy, began to feel a deep concern for the next generation of leaders for world evangelization. He began to recognize more clearly that people like his brother-in-law, Billy Graham, would have to be replaced someday, and he began a worldwide movement of finding, encouraging, equipping, and training young leaders. This vision for the future is a great blessing.

3. *Leaders should be examples in the life of the congregation.* As public figures, congregational leaders need to be models for worship, Communion participation, Bible study, prayer, and witness. They need to reflect the discipleship life. They need to reflect good stewardship of their resources.

Recently I served as consultant for a church where none of the elders attended Bible class on Sunday morning. What model of spiritual leadership is that? Leaders need to be leaders in every regard, including the spiritual life of the church.

Further, since leaders are public people, they should be above reproach. They should not be involved in any activities that could lead to a misunderstanding of their behavior or their motives. This seems unfair because other members may not be so closely scrutinized. Nevertheless, it "goes with the territory" for those who are leaders.

4. *Motivate and activate people as leaders.* Where are all the male role models? In many churches, the majority of the adults in Bible class are women. Most of the Sunday school teachers are women. The majority of the people in the choir are women. Many of those who visit the sick and the home-

bound are women. The majority of those who sit on many boards and committees are women.

I have no quarrel with women who are legitimately involved in the church's service. But how will young men get the message that they have a place in the Body of Christ? How will they understand that worship, Communion participation, Bible study, and service are part of their future life? One of the serious challenges before many churches that want to move to action is to motivate and activate the men, as well as the women, as leaders in the congregation.

5. *Sunday school teachers are some of the most important leaders in the church.* Some teachers are trained to believe that their greatest task in the Sunday school classroom is to teach the lesson. It isn't. Their greatest task is to be kind, loving, warm, friendly people who impart a love for Jesus and an enthusiasm for his mission. That's what is most important about Sunday school teaching.

Did you go to Sunday school as a young person? Do you remember any of your teachers by name? If you do, can you reflect on the subject matter and the style of teaching of just one lesson? Probably not. Do you remember the teacher's love and enthusiasm and excitement? Do you remember his or her smile? Do you remember when you got into trouble and the teacher taught you what forgiveness is all about?

In addition to the emphasis on the lesson, the doctrine, and the techniques, Sunday school training should emphasize the teacher as a Christian person and role model.

6. *Since teenagers are at an extremely critical point in life, it is important that adults, as Christian role models and leaders, spend time with them.* The youth are often a forgotten group in the congregation. They are certainly a challenge, and ministry to youth does require much time and energy. But good, wholesome role models are vitally important to this age group.

7. *The pastor and lay leaders should spend significant time with youth and adults who are potential church workers.* The leaders can have a great influence on those who feel called

to full-time service. They need to let these people into their private worlds. The youth need to be able to see the good and the bad, the positive and the negative aspects of ministry. Both youth and adult potential church workers will be making significant decisions about their lives. They will be investing great amounts of time, effort, and money in their training. They need to know as much as possible about what it really means to be in full-time service to Christ.

LEADERSHIP IN THE HOME

Christian leadership begins in the home. According to God's order of creation, the father is the head of the household. In single-parent families, God gives special strength and power to the single parent. My paternal grandfather died when my father was a young boy. He and his two brothers were raised by a mother who had to be both mother and father to the children. My grandmother saw that they were raised with the Bible in their hands and Christ in their hearts.

Under normal circumstances, God has provided children with both a father and a mother in the house. Fathers are to be the spiritual leaders. But the position of spiritual leadership has been abdicated by many men and has almost come to be stereotyped as "women's work." If anyone prays with the children at bedtime, it is usually the mother. The mother is often the one who leads the family devotions. If the Christian church is going to move into the age of action, it will need sound leadership. If the church is going to have sound leadership, fathers need to take their God-given responsibility as leaders in the home.

In the past, denominations have often recruited missionaries by showing films that share testimonies of missionaries to students who are studying for full-time church work. But if the church wants missionaries in the next generation to meet the challenge for world evangelization, parents need to be telling their six-year-olds about world evangelization today. If a church wants to transform the attitudes of its members so that they understand discipleship and mission, the place to begin is with the children at home.

If the church wants workers who are committed to a full-time vocation of serving Christ, it is essential that parents do not get caught up in the habit of going to church and returning home to have "roast preacher" for lunch. Little children have big ears, and they understand far more than parents usually realize. An important part of parental leadership is to be cautious about talking about church problems in front of children. When this happens, parents are planting seeds. They are leading, but they are leading badly.

The coming generations of Christians may be the key to world evangelization and the fulfillment of the Lord's Great Commission to make disciples of all peoples. It is important to develop attitudes in the home among small children and plant the seeds of the church in action that will bear fruit for discipleship and mission in generations to come.

Motivating Leadership

Leadership provides motivation. Proper motivation in the church is vital. Some leaders try to motivate by the Law. They put pressure on others to do certain things. They try to manipulate people. They try to make them feel guilty. They "twist arms" to get a job done. That kind of leadership doesn't work in the church. People in God's kingdom are motivated by the gospel.

Here is an example of motivation by the Law: "The Lord Jesus Christ gave the Great Commission. It is not his suggestion; it is his command. If you are to be obedient to Jesus Christ, then you must be about the business of making disciples. Further, would you like to have it on your conscience that people are dying and going to hell? How would you like to be standing next to someone on Judgment Day and have him ask you, 'Why didn't you tell me about Jesus Christ? Now I'm going to go to hell for eternity. We were friends for years. Why didn't you tell me?' "

Here is an example of motivation by the gospel: "God, by his grace in Jesus Christ, has given us the wonderful gift of forgiveness and new life. We are baptized. We are free to live as his people. We are privileged to be in partnership in his mission—the greatest adventure human beings can know. What an opportunity we have to share the gospel with other people! Think of it! Think of Judgment Day! Suppose there was someone standing next to you—someone who looked somewhat familiar, but you couldn't really remember who he was—and he were to say to you, 'It's because of you that I will share eternity with Jesus Christ. Remember me? Thirty years ago you were kind to me, helped me, and shared with me the good news about Jesus Christ.' What a wonderful privilege and honor that God would use us as channels through whom he would change the eternal destiny of those for whom Jesus died on the cross!"

There is nothing untruthful in either approach. But it is the gospel that properly stimulates people to action. God's promises give us a power that God's commands and threats, because of our sin, can never provide. The Spirit of Jesus, who brings us to faith in the good news of forgiveness also gives us power through our trusting in those promises to lead a dynamic and fruitful life.

A useful motivational technique for Christian leaders is the self-fulfilling prophecy. Self-fulfilling prophecy holds out a positive expectation of those who are your followers. It is empowering, directing, and encourages them to fulfill that expectation.

For example, psychologists have proved that a young person who is constantly told as a child that he is "stupid" will not only grow up thinking that he is stupid, but he will probably score lower than his classmates on academic achievement tests. Why? Because he is fulfilling the expectation that was set before him by some inappropriate leadership.

Self-fulfilling prophecy can be an effective and positive means of motivation in the church. For example, what if an elder had the responsibility to encourage members of the church to welcome visitors? Suppose this elder had the task of presenting the announcements in church before the worship service. He has two choices for motivating the people. He could say, "I would like all of you who are visitors to raise your hands so that we can identify you and share a packet of information with you about our church. While the ushers are passing out that information, I would like to extend a welcome to you. And as a message to all of our members, I hope that you will also welcome these people after the worship service. Take a little time, go over and see these people, introduce yourselves, and get to know our visitors." That is a paternalistic and condescending style of leadership motivation.

Using self-fulfilling prophecy, the elder can accomplish the same thing in a more positive way. It would sound something like this: "We welcome our visitors today. If you would just raise your hands, we would like to see who you are and say a word of welcome. While the ushers are bringing you a packet of information about our church, I want to share with you how thankful we are that you are worshiping here with us today. You will discover that our church is one of the friendliest churches you have ever attended. Don't be surprised if many people from our congregation come up and introduce themselves to you after the worship service. You will find that this is indeed a friendly church."

The practice of self-fulfilling prophecy places a high value on the individual. This reflects how Jesus Christ values people. His last words on earth were a self-fulfilling prophecy of high expectation for his people. He said, "You will be my witnesses in Jerusalem, and in all Judea and Samaria, and to the ends of the earth" (Acts 1:8).

TEN CHARACTERISTICS OF QUALITY LEADERSHIP

The church that wants to move into the age of action needs quality leadership. At least ten features describe quality Christian leadership.

1. *Spiritual commitment.* Christian leaders, lay and pastoral, are not only leaders of particular tasks, roles, or jobs in the church. They need to be Spirit-filled leaders in word and deed. Their lifestyles should reflect a solid commitment to Jesus Christ as Savior and Lord.

That doesn't mean that leaders must be perfect. They celebrate the forgiveness of Jesus Christ. As they participate in the Lord's Supper, they witness their hunger and thirst for righteousness. They demonstrate their source of new life in Jesus Christ and his cross.

2. *Student of the Word.* Christian leaders are involved with the Word of God. Quality Christian leadership sees the Bible not only as an academic resource but also as the power of their salvation and a blueprint for living. Christian leaders put high value on the Word, not only in theory but also in practice. Theologically, the Bible is the Word of God. It is authoritative. It does not contain errors. It is God's inspired Word.

In practice, the Bible is a tool for everyday use. It is not just "the book the preacher uses for preaching," or the book that looks nice on the coffee table. For the leader, the Bible is a daily companion. It is treated and honored in a sacred way. How is that? It is underlined. The corners of the pages are bent. Paper clips have torn the pages at the top. Notes are scribbled in the margins. The covers are worn. As the sword of the Spirit (Eph. 6:17), it's a well-worn weapon.

The leader is involved in the Word in a number of ways: in

worship and Communion attendance, in weekly structured Bible study with the congregation, and in personal Bible study as part of the devotional life and with the family.

3. *Dreamer and visionary.* Quality Christian leaders expect great things from a great God. Leaders are dreamers of what God can accomplish. They stretch the horizons of those who follow. They constantly lift up challenges and opportunities and inspire other leaders to trust God and use their resources so those dreams may become realities. Leaders attempt great things for God. They believe in the words "I would rather attempt great things and fail than attempt nothing and succeed."

4. *Motivator and equipper.* Quality leaders motivate others. They encourage, equip, and direct them. They would rather motivate three people to do a task in twenty minutes than accomplish it themselves in ten minutes. They would rather motivate others not because they are lazy, but because they see the involvement of others as a ministry to them.

5. *Edifier.* Quality Christian leaders are also edifying people. They are not critical or punitive in their leadership. They build others up in their faith, encourage them, and make them feel better about their life in Jesus Christ.

6. *Optimistic.* Leaders are filled with optimism. They recognize that faith is sure about things we do not see (Heb. 11:1). It is clear to them that in all things God works for the good of those who love him (Rom. 8:28). This optimism, like the apostle Paul's, is in Christ: "I can do everything through him who gives me strength" (Phil. 4:13). Such leaders exude that optimism and infect others with it. They put the best construction on everything. When some say that the glass is half empty, optimistic leaders remind them that it is half full. When the day is partly cloudy, they point out that it is mostly sunny. When someone emphasizes a negative aspect of another person, they are quick to call attention to the positive qualities of that person.

7. *A servant.* Servant leadership is the style of the Scrip-

tures. Jesus said that the one who wants to be first must be last. Whoever wants to be a leader must be a slave of the rest (Mark 10:43-45).

In the Christian life there can be false pride, and there can be genuine pride. False pride looks at self and takes pride in what is really God's gift (Luke 18:19). Genuine pride looks at Christ, his forgiveness, and the new life that he imparts with his forgiveness. The leader knows the difference. The leader boasts, "I no longer live, but Christ lives in me" (Gal. 2:20a).

Likewise, in the Christian life there can be false humility, and there can be genuine humility. False humility says, "I am worth nothing; there is nothing I can accomplish, nothing I can do." True humility says, "Without Christ I can do nothing. But with Christ I can do everything." The leader knows the difference and demonstrates true humility.

8. *A people person.* Quality Christian leaders are people persons. It seems as though the world consists of two kinds of people—"people persons" and "thing persons." Some people are geared to work with others. They relate well and feel comfortable with people, and people respond to them. They are people persons. Other people have been designed to work with things. It doesn't mean that they are hermits. They still relate to some people. They marry and have children. They have friends. But they don't spend most of their vocational life or their Christian service life working with people. They would rather work with things. These people are good with their hands, good with their minds. They are the accountants, trustees, electricians, scientists, and architects. Some people are both people persons and thing persons. The quality Christian leader must be a people person.

As a pastor, I once had a student worker from the seminary. Bill was a fine guy. He had a nice wife, and they were genuinely committed Christians. Bill was very intelligent as well. But in the pulpit he was a nervous wreck. He made the shut-ins age years during his visits. They were on the edge of their seats and complained about how awkward he seemed. At first, I thought it was a case of inexperience, but as a full year went by there was no improvement. At church on Sunday, he just didn't seem to know what to say or how to interact with people, either formally or informally.

One day I sat down with Bill. We prayed, and we talked about his intentions to enter the ministry. I asked him why he wanted to become a pastor. He said that he wasn't really sure he wanted to be one. It was his mother who wanted him to be a pastor. I asked him what he would like to do if he could have any vocation. He said that he would like to work for the forestry service or be a mail carrier. What wonderful occupations! What great ways to serve God and to serve people! But a people person? Bill wasn't that. A quality Christian leader needs to be a people-oriented individual.

9. *Passionate for the lost.* Quality leaders have a passion for those who are lost. Jesus said, "If anyone would come after me, he must deny himself and take up his cross and follow me" (Matt. 16:24). From this, many in the church have developed a "theology of the cross" that stresses the passion and the suffering of Jesus. Indeed, that is the servant side of the quality leader. It includes sacrifice—perhaps even of one's life—as we complete the sufferings of Christ (Rom. 8:17; Phil. 3:10). We are to have the same humility in suffering that Christ did. The apostle Paul makes this clear in Philippians 2:5-8: "Your attitude should be the same as that of Christ Jesus: Who, being in very nature God, did not consider equality with God something to be grasped, but made himself nothing, taking the very nature of a servant, being made in human likeness. And being found in appearance as a man, he humbled himself and became obedient to death—even death on a cross!" That is the suffering and the humility side of the theology of the cross.

But there is another side to the theology of the cross—namely, the reason Jesus was there at Calvary. It is the mis-

sion side of the cross. A theology of the cross is incom
without the mission.

Paul makes clear the mission side of the cross in this p
sage: "Therefore God exalted him to the highest place and
gave him the name that is above every name, that at the
name of Jesus every knee should bow, in heaven and on
earth and under the earth, and every tongue confess that
Jesus Christ is Lord, to the glory of God the Father" (Phil.
2:9-11).

The meritorious work of the cross is to reach all people so
that in honor of the name of Jesus they will openly proclaim
that Jesus Christ is Lord. This is the fulfillment of the Great
Commission. This is the mission side of the cross. This is the
passion for the lost that drove Jesus to the cross. When Jesus
calls us to take up our cross and follow him (Matt. 16:24), he
is also saying, "Take on that passion for those who are lost."
The quality leader has that passion.

10. *Tenacious.* Quality Christian leaders don't give up.
With the patience of Job, the strong Christian leader hangs
in there when everyone else would have given up. The root
of the biblical word for "leader" carries the strong connota-
tion of perseverance. Every leader whom God chooses
seems to go through a difficult time. It almost seems to be
necessary by God's design. God's people literally went
through the desert before they reached the promised land.

Every leader seems to have a desert story to tell. Perhaps
it is a time of testing, an adventure in maturity, and experience in trusting God. During that time, the leader turns to
God and learns the depth and breadth of what it means to
rely on God's power for deliverance and peace, for strength
and endurance. The leader often learns this in a way that
otherwise would have been impossible to experience. The
great Christian leader Paul wrote: "We have this treasure in
jars of clay to show that this all-surpassing power is from
God and not from us. We are hard pressed on every side,
but not crushed; perplexed, but not in despair; persecuted,

but not abandoned; struck down, but not destroyed" (2 Cor. 4:7-9). Quality leaders have learned—often the hard way— to hang in there.

TWO KINDS OF LEADERSHIP

There are two kinds of leadership: authoritarian and servant. Jesus identified the difference between the two when he told the disciples, "You know that those who are regarded as rulers of the Gentiles lord it over them, and their high officials exercise authority over them. Not so with you. Instead, whoever wants to become great among you must be your servant, and whoever wants to be first must be slave of all. For even the Son of Man did not come to be served, but to serve, and to give his life as a ransom for many" (Mark 10:42-45).

Authoritarian leadership is a controlling leadership. It must be in charge of everything. It lacks a trust in God, who is ultimately in control of everything. This leader assumes control as a demonstration of lack of faith.

Authoritarian leadership is paternalistic, overbearing, and protecting to the extent that it limits the possibilities of those who follow. It creates a dependence on its leadership. It never allows followers the strength, power, knowledge, or opportunities to excel beyond the position of the leader. It keeps followers "in their places."

Authoritarian leadership is condescending. The leader looks down on the followers, feeling that the leader's office and title are more important than the personal development of the followers or the fulfillment of the group's goals.

The authoritarian is highly concerned with gaining and keeping power and authority. This type of leader gives followers only those resources that will clearly not threaten the power and the authority that the leader holds.

Authoritarians are distant. They tend to put themselves

on a pedestal. Therefore, among the followers, they are not genuine. They hide behind the mask of their office and play games through the facade of leadership.

Authoritarians are concerned first and foremost with the preservation of the institution because it maintains the security of their leadership. Consequently, they are only secondarily concerned with the group's goals and are unlikely to take risks or experiment.

As described above, authoritarian leadership is contrary to the biblical models of discipleship, contrary to the kind of love that God has for his people, as well as the power that God gives his people through the Holy Spirit.

Servant leadership has been transformed by the power of the gospel and finds its identity in Jesus Christ, who came to serve. It is also *transforming* leadership in that it seeks to be involved in significant, radical, and basic change, bringing the followers and others more and more into connection with the transforming power of the gospel of Jesus.

Servant leadership does not ask the followers to glorify the leader, but points them to Christ, the true Servant Leader. Relying on Christ and his promises enables the followers to reach their God-given potential. Christ-centered leadership builds up and supports others, lifts them up in encouragement and in prayer to God, and seeks to train them—even to the extent that they may surpass the leader, if that is God's will. Servant leaders are not insecure about their positions because their security is not tied to the institution but to the Body of Christ, to a divine calling, and to the power of Pentecost.

The servant leader is a true servant of others. Unlike the authoritarian, the servant leader does not try to lord it over the followers and has truly come not to be served, but to serve.

Servant leaders are genuine. They are transparent, willing to share their weaknesses and strengths, their joys and sorrows; willing to laugh and to cry with their followers. Their sense of stability is not centered in their own empire, for their Kingdom and security are not of this world.

Above all else, servant leaders are concerned with the mission of God, and not about making a living. *They are called to make a difference.* They understand that at the cross of the Christian life are the words of Paul: "Do not conform any longer to the pattern of this world, but be transformed by the renewing of your mind" (Rom. 12:2). Therefore servant leaders offer themselves as living sacrifices to God, dedicated to his service and pleasing to him (v. 1).

Quality leadership is one of God's greatest gifts for the congregation that wants to go through the servant change to become a church in action. Leadership is a key for moving a church. Pray for your leadership. Encourage and support your leaders. Invest in your leaders with your time, your energy, and your money. They are God's gift to your church, and they are essential for moving your church to action. The most important leaders of all are the pastors. They are the subject of the next chapter.

Discussion Questions

1. Can you clearly differentiate between leader and manager in these two areas?

    a. as the secular world sees them;

    b. as the spiritual gift definitions for leadership and administration describe them.

2. Do you believe that leaders in the church are born, made, or miraculously transformed into such by God? Support your conclusion.

3. Does your church have a deliberate process of leadership training? Is this a viable alternative or supplement to determining who has the potential spiritual gift of leadership? Look back at question 2. Is what you do at your church, or what you would like to do, consistent with your view of the source of leadership?

6

The Pastor's Place in Leadership

While leadership is one of the most important components of the mix for moving the church to action, the most important individual in the leadership arena is the pastor.

There are many things to know and do as a strong pastoral leader. There are many important skills that can be learned, many of them in the academic setting. But pastors more often acquire them through reading, observation, and trial and error in the school of hard knocks. Either way, God is active in the process of developing leaders.

For many years, academicians classified leadership as a subunit of administration or management. Today the study of leadership is becoming a discipline in itself. This is primarily seen on the campuses of secular universities, especially where there is a school of business. But there is also a growing number of people who are writing and teaching the subject in Christian circles.

Many are rediscovering the leadership models provided by individuals in the Scriptures, including Jesus. Jesus' model of discipline and his command to make disciples are important. This strategy makes sense in light of Jesus' plan to reach all people and share the good news of forgiveness and new life.

The Great Commission has not remained unfulfilled because of a deficiency in God's plan and strategy, nor can it be attributed to God's lack of power. It is unfinished partly because the church has been polluted by academic intellectualism, rationalism, and institutionalism, which have led it away from the style and basic principles that Jesus modeled to his followers. Today's church is classroom-bound, whereas Jesus was relationship oriented.

There are certainly many skills and patterns that can help a pastor become the kind of leader God intended for the local flock. These skills can help the pastor develop a leadership style that moves the church to action, to mission, and ultimately to the ends of the earth. But skills and styles of ministry are not the most basic and important issues in pastoral leadership. The essential ingredient is *attitude*.

While speaking to a group of pastors and key laypeople, I explained to them the process of moving the church to action for discipleship and mission. During a break, one of the pastors approached me and asked if we could talk privately for a few moments. As we moved to a corner of the room the pastor began to explain to me why the process would not work: The people of the congregation were against anything that produced change, the pastor said. The members were self-centered and didn't care about people outside their church. The people were highly conscious of cost and would never participate in anything that would involve money.

The pastor insisted that whenever the words *evangelism* or *growth* were mentioned, it turned all the people off. "So," the pastor summarized, "something like this would never work in a church like mine for all these reasons."

I thought for a moment, and, remembering that I was from out of town and had little to lose, I decided to be brutally honest with this pastor. I responded as kindly as I could: "I see. That makes a lot of sense. But there is one other major reason why it won't work in your church."

The pastor looked at me, surprised. "What do you mean? Have you been to my church?"

"No," I responded. "I've never been to your church."

"Well, how do you know this won't work at my church? What do you mean?" the pastor inquired.

"You!" I responded. "You are the major reason why this process won't work in your church. You have a very negative opinion about the possibilities for change and growth in your church. You have a negative attitude about your people. No matter how you might try to hide that attitude, it will show. People are perceptive about these things. You are right. It won't work at your church. But the primary reason is probably you and your attitude."

God builds the church, not the pastor. But the pastor has the authority, the power, the status, and the position to frustrate and roadblock God's plan for the church more than any other individual. As the leader of the local congregation, the pastor is either the most valued asset or the greatest liability. For that reason, the training of pastors is an essential ingredient for moving a local congregation or a denomination to action.

Pastoral Training

Unfortunately, many seminaries today stress academics to such an extent that professors are attracted to seminary campuses primarily for academic reasons. Sometimes the selection of professors has little to do with their leadership abilities and their effectiveness in the practice of ministry. There are even seminaries that have a few professors who have never actually served as full-time church pastors. Consequently, role models that the students follow may exemplify an inappropriate style of leadership unless the students are planning to return to classrooms as professors. Many Bible colleges also face this same challenge.

The pastorate is one of the few occupations in which the individual moves from the classroom to the key leadership position without any steps in between. To put it in organizational language, the pastor moves from a classroom setting (usually with one year of internship) to the position of chief executive officer of a small corporation in the first year out of school. In terms of the divine call, this system can and often does work well. In terms of leadership skills and style, it is grossly unfair to the people who are called to this leadership position. It is also somewhat unkind to an unsuspecting congregation. This poor method of management (stewardship) is unparalleled in the business world, except within the family-owned business. Sometimes the heir apparent to the family business comes directly out of school and, perhaps through the untimely death of a parent, takes over the business, but this scenario often leads to the ruin of the business within five years. Nevertheless, this is the style of leadership placement in the Christian church. It is indeed miraculous that the church even survives, let alone moves forward.

God builds the church, not people. The church is called to be a good steward of the mysteries of God. That includes leadership in the pastorate. Unfortunately, many seminaries have no training or classwork in the area of leadership. If students have not had good role models of leadership in the church on the one hand, and have not had any academic leadership training on the other, even gifted pastors will invest years in trial-and-error experimentation before their leadership styles emerge and leadership skills develop.

During the last few decades, the more progressive seminaries have included courses in church administration. These courses have been helpful in preparing pastors for their administrative roles in congregations.

But until just recently, the most popular model of leadership has been that of an enabler. The enabler model reflects that the pastor is there to manage the congregation under the direction of the people. This style of leadership has been detrimental to pastoral ministry because it is a form of passive leadership. Theoretically, it sounds democratic. But it is an ineffective way for a church to operate, and it is not biblical.

The enabler model of passive leadership has resulted in

many pastors taking on a style of leadership that is reactive. They are constantly reacting to what boards and committees tell them to do. They also tend to exercise this style of leadership by reacting to the environment as well. A pastor who is in a constant state of reaction has little intentionality about the ministry. Consequently, the pastor frequently complains about spinning wheels and mending fences. If a church is going to move from the age of reaction into the age of action, the pastor must take on the biblical posture of leadership.

God calls pastors to lead. That means being out front. It requires taking the initiative. It means directing, guiding, empowering, and releasing people for their work of service. It also includes setting the vision and motivating others.

Is the pastor a leader or a manager? If the pastor is a manager, the pastor is a detail-oriented person who makes sure that everything runs smoothly. The pastor takes orders from everyone else. Boards, committees, church members, and congregational meetings set the church's agenda and write the pastor's day-to-day job description. This arrangement could work. But many of the fine Christians who sit on these boards and make these decisions are not experts about the mission of the church. As volunteers, they don't have the time to do their homework on major decisions. Many of them are not gifted leaders. Some of them are biblically illiterate. Most of all, they are not called to be God's pastoral leader in that place. When the pastor is a manager and the leadership is in the hands of a board, a committee, or the congregational meeting, the church is rendered ineffective in its mission.

When the pastor is providing transformational servant leadership, the pastor gives guidance and direction, holds forth the vision, and equips people for the work that will accomplish the goals for the church under God's blessing. This is a servant leadership, not a dictatorship.

In a small, growing congregation, the pastor may start

out as part-time manager and part-time leader. This is necessary and helpful for the growth of the fledgling congregation. But as the church grows, the pastor needs to delegate more and become more of a leader while others do the managing.

In medium-size churches, those managers may be key laypeople. Often one of them is the church secretary. Many church secretaries are the real managers of the day-to-day work of the congregation. They are perhaps some of the most underpaid and underappreciated heroes of the Christian faith.

In the larger congregation, the senior pastor is leader; other staff persons may be involved partly in leadership and partly in management. In very large congregations, all of the major professional staff members are leaders of certain areas of ministry, while executive secretaries and business managers perform the management functions.

Many churches are caught at the "200 barrier." They have averaged about two hundred people in worship for many years. Often they will grow a little and then decline. One of the reasons many churches are unable to break the 200 barrier is that the pastor is unable to give up the role of manager and shift more directly to the role of leader.

One of the key demands of the movement from manager to leader is delegation. For a pastor to emerge as a strong leader of the congregation, the pastor must learn to delegate responsibilities to others, not as a method of avoiding work, but to increase the effective impact of the congregation. This is often hard for a pastor who has served a smaller congregation from the beginning and has always been tempted to do everything. As the congregation grows, it is a real challenge for the pastor to change styles of ministry.

Further, in many denominations there is a counterproductive pattern in which pastors move from smaller churches to larger churches. It is generally thought that if a pastor is effective in a smaller church, the pastor will jump at the chance to take a call to a larger church. The typical "career" pattern for a pastor is to progress from smaller churches to larger churches. This counterproductive pattern brings a pastor with a small-church mentality into a large-church setting. The result is frustration for both the pastor and the congregation.

If a pastor were to move from a larger congregation to a smaller church, and if the pastor had learned good leadership skills and delegation patterns, then the large-church mentality would help the smaller church to grow faster. But the movement of a pastor from a large church to a smaller church is rare, except perhaps when a pastor approaches retirement. Otherwise, when it does happen, many of the pastor's colleagues wonder what was done wrong to deserve the "demotion."

The multiple staff of a large church provides an excellent opportunity for a pastor to be mentored under a senior pastor in the styles of leadership that are positive and helpful. As an assistant pastor develops a leadership style, the style can be refined by growing with the multiple staff as the congregation grows. Or, the pastor can move that style to a smaller congregation, bringing both the style and the large-church mentality to that setting. This would help many churches break the 200 barrier in which they have been trapped for years.

THE GREAT MIX-UP

One of the greatest deterrents to moving the church to action is a reversal of roles between the pastor and the people. When this happens, the pastor serves in a role of one-on-one personal ministry while the people serve in a leadership role. C. Peter Wagner has dealt with this thoroughly in his brilliant book *Leading Your Church to Growth* (Ventura, Calif.: Regal Books, 1984).

Wagner points out that as the role of the pastor as the

lone one-on-one minister expands and the role of the people as leader increases, the effectiveness, vitality, and
growth of the church decline. On the other hand, as the role
of the pastor as leader expands and the role of the people as
servants of Christ and of their neighbors increases, the
vitality, health, and growth of the church expand.

Wagner's point is that God has designed the church to be
a body of believers who are involved in ministry. The word
ministry means "service." Every Christian, as a temple of
the Holy Spirit, with the Spirit's gifts, is called to be
engaged in Christian service—that is, service to others. Pastors have their role as ministers of the Word of God.
Laypeople have their role as fellow-servants to each other
and to their neighbor. As Peter says (1 Pet. 2:4-5, 9-10), the
whole body of Christian believers is a holy priesthood,
called to reflect in their lives the holiness and love of God
and to declare the praises of God, who has shown them
mercy. This body of believers has a proper function of ministry (i.e., service). They call a pastoral leader to equip them
for ministry by proclaiming to them God's Word and
administering the sacraments God has instituted. This is a
discipleship model. Ephesians 4 clearly indicates that the
people of God are to serve, and those whom God has called
as pastors are to equip the people for this work of service.

Of course, the pastor is never removed entirely from one-
on-one ministry to people. The pastor still makes calls,
counsels, visits, teaches, and preaches. Nor are the people
limited in such a way that they are not involved at all in
leadership. These are not absolutes, but as more people
become involved in service and fewer in leadership, and as
the pastor tends to be more involved in leadership guided
by God's Word, the church is more apt to move to action. It
is more likely to be a vital congregation that makes disciples
and moves out in mission. This makes sense because it is
God's design for the relationship of the office of the public
ministry and the priesthood of all believers.

This style of leadership is sensitive to two important biblical principles: First, when the pastor is equipping the people to do the work of Christ, the aim is a multiplication of service in the Body of Christ. This multiplication is God's key strategy for the fulfillment of the Great Commission to make disciples of all peoples. Pastors are not going to fulfill the Great Commission by themselves (Acts 6). Second, this strategy is sensitive to God's gracing his church with spiritual gifts. The pastor does not have all the spiritual gifts necessary to meet the needs that God has placed before the church. But the people collectively do have all the gifts of grace that God deems necessary to meet the needs God has put before the church.

Many churches have completely reversed God's plan for the church. Some people believe that only the pastor can visit someone in the hospital, that only an ordained clergyman can counsel someone who needs biblical direction, that only a pastor can conduct a Bible study or lead a devotion or pray, and that only the laity can lead and direct the business and the program of the local church.

The biblical model is that the entire Body of Christ does the work of service that the Lord prepared for them to do. The pastor's ministry is called to equip the people for their "ministry," so that the work of making disciples can be accomplished. Many pastors spend their days running from hospital to hospital, from shut-in visit to shut-in visit, from Bible study to Bible study. Meanwhile, too many laypeople spend agonizing hours in meetings trying to make leadership decisions for which they are neither trained nor qualified. Reversing this mix-up releases the pastor for leadership and the body of believers for service in ways that will move the church to action. Rearranging the great mix-up would have quite an impact on how many pastors and lay leaders spend their days. Instead of attending meetings, laypeople would be doing ministry. Much more ministry would be accomplished. Further, the pastor's job description would change. The pastor would again be equipping God's people for "the work of the ministry" (Eph. 4:12 KJV) by planning and shaping the church's ministry and deploying its people into service.

To the surprise of many pastors, one of the most important functions of their work would be reading "junk mail." Many pastors loathe reading this kind of mail. But if they see themselves as equippers of the saints, they are the ones who need to delegate and direct specific information that comes through the mail to the appropriate people in the congregation. The pastor can be the bottleneck or can be the funnel through which people are exposed to the latest best thinking in Christian ministry.

The pastor as leader should spend time daydreaming. Constructive daydreaming seeks God's vision for the mission of the church; it develops plans and strategies, it sees possibilities and stretches the horizons. Every pastor should spend some good quality time daydreaming every week.

The pastor as leader is a self-starter. The pastor is not reactionary but actionary, not responding to the environment nor mending fences. The pastor is designing and building; not putting out fires, but leading people. The pastor as leader must take this initiative. In this sense, the pastor is aggressive, not passive. But the pastor is not a dictator. Good leaders understand the dynamics of process decision making. People should never be surprised about decisions. To put it another way, there should never be a negative vote about an important issue at a congregational meeting. Nor should a major issue be decided by a small margin of votes.

A close vote or a "no" vote reflects the absence of process decision making: Either people don't understand the issue well enough, and it has not been processed in their minds long enough; or, it is not God's will.

Here is where good pastoral and lay leadership can work

in partnership. If the pastor and lay leaders process an issue through the people carefully over a period of time, there should be no surprises about the outcome of a decision. This type of decision making indicates a strong sense of leadership but rejects a dictatorial tone to that leadership. This kind of leadership helps to move a church to action.

TWO ABUSES OF PASTORAL LEADERSHIP

Two abuses of pastoral leadership are found in many churches today.

1. *Some pastors hide behind the office or the call to the pastoral ministry.* Though the call to the ministry is ordained by God, no pastor has the right to be ineffective. The call to the ministry does not excuse laziness or mediocrity. Nor does it preclude the possibility that someone is misplaced or unqualified for the ministry.

Some pastors are just not suited for the pastoral ministry. They may know Greek and Hebrew and can be soundly orthodox, but that does not guarantee that they will never become a millstone around the neck of a congregation. Therefore, it is inappropriate for a pastor to hide behind the office or the call and pretend that the results of that ministry make no difference. Of course the results of ministry matter! That is what stewardship of the gospel is all about.

2. *The opposite is also an abuse.* That is the growing phenomenon of deteriorating respect for the pastoral office and its authority, and the lack of clarity about the call to the ministry. There has been a recent trend for pastors to be treated more and more like employees and for laypeople even to talk about hiring and firing pastors just as they would refer to an employee at work. This abuse parallels the deteriorating respect for authority in the world today. But it is also nurtured by pastors who have a limited model

of pastoral leadership or who have operated in ministry as hourly employees.

A related issue is what C. Peter Wagner calls "follower-ship." One of the greatest needs in many congregations is for instruction in what it means to be a follower as part of God's order of creation. God is a God of order. He has established an order in the world and in the church. Just as children are to respect the position of their parents, so the people of a congregation should respect the pastor, the undershepherd of the flock. This respect for the pastor does not excuse ineffectiveness or allow for special privileges. Leadership is a matter of responsibilities, not privileges; fol-lowership respects leadership.

Some have confused the proper issues of leadership and followership with issues about the erosion of the pastoral office. They think sharing ministry with laypeople is an ero-sion of pastoral authority. In reality, sharing is the biblical pattern. It relates to the scriptural principle that as you give away, you receive, and as you lose, you gain. The apostle Paul, after all, described lay Christians as his fellow work-ers. The key to leadership is not in overprotection of the office, but in a clear understanding of the call, based on a view of God's relationship to the Body of Christ; God's placement of a leader in relationship to the followers; and the equipping of God's people, his holy priesthood, for their work of service.

DYNAMIC LEADERSHIP

What kind of pastoral leadership is needed to move the church to action? What makes an effective pastor?

First, let's consider what does not make an effective pastor.

1. *Education does not necessarily make an effective pastor.* Many ineffective pastors are highly educated. Many strong-

ly effective pastors have little education. Education is not a key factor.

2. *The pastor's personality is not a fundamental factor for effective leadership.* God uses many different personalities in powerful ways for the leadership of his kingdom. Many people believe that if their pastor only had the Hollywood glitter of some of the clergy they see on television, their church would be led effectively. That is just not so.

3. *Certain spiritual gifts are not what make a pastor an effective leader.* Yes, there is a gift of leadership. Pastors with that gift tend to assume roles of leadership more easily within the church. But there are those who do not have the gift of leadership. They have learned to exercise the role of leadership and to use whatever other gifts they have for effective leadership.

Many scholars believe that pastors with certain gifts are less likely to be effective leaders of large or growing congregations. These gifts include pastoring (shepherding), mercy, and service; they generally tend to reflect a one-on-one ministry. This approach to the pastoral ministry may well serve a smaller congregation, but the leader of a larger congregation usually cannot spend a lot of time meeting with people one-on-one (unless discipling a few people on a personal basis). In this sense, the pastor, as leader, needs to be more goal oriented than relationship oriented.

There are at least twelve aspects or characteristics of leadership in general that also apply to the pastor as leader:

1. *Focus.* Effective leaders have learned how to focus their lives. They are not dabbling in dozens of pursuits, rendering themselves watered down to a level of ineffectiveness. Strong leaders know their priorities and follow them. Consequently, good leaders know how to say no. Effective leaders focus their energies.

2. *Vision.* Effective leaders have a vision of what can be accomplished and share that vision with others to the

extent that others take ownership in it and claim it as their own. This means that good leaders are often strongly conceptual. It also means that they are good communicators and can clearly help others catch the vision.

3. *Processors.* Effective leaders understand life as a process. They are skilled at processing information through other people. They do not see people as static but constantly growing. They see the church as a movement rather than a stultified entity. They see life as a progression rather than an event.

4. *Goals.* Effective leaders set goals for themselves and create goals for the group. They are, therefore, future oriented. They remember the past and try to learn from it, but only as a means to a greater end: accomplishing the mission set before them. As goal setters, they are constantly creating strategies to achieve those goals and regularly taking inventory to determine whether or not those goals are being achieved.

5. *Discipline.* Effective leaders are disciplined. They often work while others play. Yet they keep a proper balance between recreation and work. Effective leaders demonstrate self-control in budgeting their time. They discipline their activities, becoming involved in those activities that help accomplish their goals and resisting involvements that would clutter their lives.

6. *Jugglers.* Effective leaders are good jugglers. They can keep twelve balls in the air at the same time. It takes a special kind of person to have several issues to deal with at any given time and not lose track of them or let them "fall through the cracks."

7. *Growth.* Effective leaders have the desire to grow, coupled with the pursuit of excellence. They have a deep aspiration to move forward. This is reflected in a passion for personal growth, as well as for the growth of the church.

8. *Sacrifice.* Effective leaders know what it means to sacrifice. A large part of leadership is just plain hard work. There

is a certain energy about the leader that is powerful and inspires others. They are sacrificial in that they deny themselves pleasures or opportunities that detract from the task at hand.

9. *Mission.* Effective leaders are committed to the mission they have. They are not off on some tangent or flitting from one fad to another.

10. *Change.* Effective leaders are open to change. This openness is not a disregard for evaluating the appropriateness of change nor an openness to change for change's sake. Nevertheless, when change is important, necessary, or helpful, effective leaders are open to it for themselves personally and for the church.

11. *Eclectic.* Effective leaders are not so self-centered or independent that they cannot accept help from the outside. Many pastors believe that they have to invent everything themselves. One might call these pastors "prima donnas." They constantly have to "do their own thing." Although originality is helpful, too much innovation and spontaneity can reflect an impulsiveness that brings disorder and chaos to the church. Innovation from the inside only breeds blind spots to what God is doing elsewhere. Many churches today reflect positive, effective leadership that is eclectic as pastors more often seek the services of an outside, objective consultant.

12. *Tenacity.* Effective leaders do not give up in tough times. They press on toward the goal. Sir Winston Churchill, in an address to the student body at a school he had attended as a youth, gave his entire speech in one short line: "Never, never, never, never, never, give up." For Churchill, these words were not just rhetoric. His life story is an amazing example of a leader who would not give up, leading a nation that would not give up. Pastors with that kind of tenacity make effective leaders.

LONG-TERM PASTORATES

Some pastors have the idea that they should change congregations and move on every few years. Some denominations even require that pastors move frequently. Generally, this is counterproductive for the church that wants to move forward to action.

A church that changes pastors every few years can at least be guaranteed that it will never have any long-term goals. John had been pastor of his congregation for more than fourteen years. He did a fine job of ministry. Two years ago John reached retirement age, but he was unsure if he really wanted to retire completely from the ministry. His wife urged him to do so, but he liked the people, and the people certainly liked him. Leaving the congregation would be a difficult adjustment. He kept putting off a decision. He had made an arrangement with the elders that on December 1 of every year he would tell them whether he would continue for one more year. This arrangement made it almost impossible for the congregation to set any long-term goals or even know beyond twelve months into the future who the pastor would be. Just the possibility of change caused his ministry to be somewhat ineffective.

Many pastors leave a church before they reach their peak of effectiveness. The first year is the honeymoon year. The pastor is just finding his/her way around. Everybody likes the pastor, and they accept just about anything suggested. During the second and third years, the "alligators" in the congregation come out of the tall bushes and begin to show their teeth. The luster is worn off the new pastor, and the people are beginning to see weaknesses. In the fourth and fifth years the alligators start to bite. This is a difficult time in a pastor's life. Congregations often lose their leaders at this point. The sad part is that the alligators are usually a small minority, but the majority of the people are often silent. They need to come to the aid of the pastor, and when they don't, the pastor often begins to consider other alternatives. Then when the pastor does accept a call, the majority of the people are awestruck that the pastor is leaving them.

However, in those cases where the pastor "hangs in there" and the majority gives its support, the alligators discover that they can't push the pastor out (as they did the last one). In about the sixth year, the alligators either begin to look for another swamp (their view of church) or they become bullfrogs. As bullfrogs, they hop around a little and sometimes make a croaking noise, but generally they are quite harmless. In about the seventh year, the pastor's most productive time in ministry begins.

MULTIPLE STAFF

Many churches that are stuck in the maintenance rut got that way largely because they are understaffed. There are two common causes of understaffing, and both have to do with money. (But the money is a symptom, not a cause.) One cause is overbuilding, and the other is continuing a particular ministry that is oversubsidized. (Often this is an elementary school in those denominations that have such schools.) This is not a criticism of buildings or elementary schools. Both are important parts of the church's ministry. The issue here is that the congregation has overbuilt or oversubsidized just one facet. It is a matter of degree.

Generally, as churches consider their assets, they tend to overvalue bricks and mortar and undervalue good pastoral staff. A rule of thumb for staffing a vital congregation that is moving in discipleship and mission is one pastor (or professional staff person) for every two hundred to two hundred and fifty people in worship. Many congregations staff at the wrong time because they do not understand staffing for growth. Instead of staffing for growth, churches often staff because of growth. When a church staffs because of growth, it will reach four hundred members, and suddenly someone will say, "If we don't get another pastor, Pastor Jones is going to die of a heart attack." Then the church gets another pastor.

Staffing for growth means that when a congregation reaches two hundred to two hundred and fifty in worship, it will add staff to generate further growth. One style of staffing is reactionary. The other is actionary staffing by anticipation. Staffing for growth requires risk and a certain amount of faith. Many churches have a thermometer chart at the entrance that depicts a fund drive for a building. Rarely does one see a fund drive aimed at gathering money for a new staff person. Churches generally think more about bricks and mortar than they do about quality staff.

What about staffing a church when a Christian school is part of the ministry? If a church has a Christian school, count each teacher as a minus one-tenth pastor. In other words, if a congregation had one pastor and ten teachers, it would really be a congregation staffed with zero pastors.

When a congregation has a Christian school, many people believe that the teachers ought to "count for something" in the pastoral ministry. But if those teachers are conducting a proper ministry of service to children in the classroom and to the children's families, they have a full-time job with their own "congregations." Further, if the Christian school is tied to the overall ministry of the church, it actually demands more time of the pastor because, as a priority, the pastor must also minister to the school staff and its needs. The size of the school, reflected in the number of teachers, determines the demand on the pastor. Therefore, the staffing rule of thumb is to subtract one-tenth of a pastor for every teacher.

Should a congregation have a senior minister or associate pastors? The model of associate (or "equal") pastors is usually a serious mistake. Even where such arrangements exist, there is really only one head pastor. A sign is commonly found on the desks of leaders that reads: "The buck stops here." It simply means that the responsibility ultimately has to converge on one person. It cannot fall on two people, such as two supposedly equal associate pastors.

A recent development in staffing that has good biblical basis involves specialization in certain areas of ministry on the basis of spiritual gifts. People used to think that if a pastor didn't preach, something was wrong. Every pastor had to preach in order to be a "real pastor." Many people simply call the pastor "Preacher."

Today the trend is to place people in ministry according to their gifts. This means that in some churches there are assistant pastors who rarely preach (for example, only when the senior minister is away). This makes sense because congregations tend to relate well to one person. Some churches that have a multiple staff in which a number of pastors are gifted preachers also have multiple services. Each pastor has a "congregation" (based on the time of service) where that pastor will be the senior minister—the preacher—for that group of people.

Another staffing trend that is becoming common among servant leaders is the development, deployment, and commissioning of laypeople from the congregation to serve as full-time staff workers. This is a good system for at least five reasons.

• Laypeople have an opportunity to serve full time without having to move to another city, quit their jobs, and acquire several years of expensive college or seminary training.

• Many of these people, after a few years of active service on such a staff, may be able to go to college or seminary anyway. This often happens as parents experience the empty-nest syndrome. Those who pursue a college or seminary education do so as well-informed students, having served on the staff for several years.

• Staffing from the congregation helps the denomination because it does not drain the supply of pastors and other church workers. This leaves pastors within the denomination available for church planting and other ministries.

• This strategy provides a model for others in the congregation to consider full-time work within their own church.

• Staffing from within the congregation also promotes a smooth transition for church expansion. Those who leave their secular jobs and begin full-time employment with the congregation already know its philosophy of mission and service. They also know the pastor, other staff members, and the people. Further, there is no cost for moving new staff members in, and the people themselves do not have to relocate.

LEADERSHIP IS KEY

Behind every movement, local or worldwide, there is a "fanatic," someone who is a key leader, who pours his or her life into the task. In the church that key person is the pastor. When there is a multiple staff, that key person must be the senior pastor.

It is not a matter of doing God's job, building his kingdom, or moving his church. It's a matter of being willing and open to let God be God in and through his people in the congregation. The actionary church and the servant leader seek God's will, rely on God's Word, and depend on God's promises. Through the power of God's Word and promises they respond to the call to be disciples and to make disciples.

Discussion Questions

1. In his book *Leading Your Church to Growth*, C. Peter Wagner states that there are two pastoral dilemmas: "being

both humble and powerful, and being both a servant and a leader." What do you think Wagner means by these apparent contradictions?

2. Discuss the relative merits of role modeling, formal education, and on-the-job training as they affect leadership ability and style.

3. Outline a process of leadership training for your church. Consider who could perform any of the functions suggested in question 2, as well as scriptural justification for each element of your training and adherence to the integrity of the Great Commission.

4. (For laypeople only) Carefully analyze (without the use of a stopwatch and efficiency expert) how much of your pastor's time is spent on ministry to people that could just as effectively be performed by others and how much is spent equipping the saints to do this and other ministry. Is this a fair balance?

5. Discuss the statement: "There should never be a negative vote about an important issue at a congregational meeting." Is this a proper statement, in your judgment? Why or why not? List the reasons that negative votes may have occurred in your church.

6. You may wish to do some research on what leadership and "followership" entail. Based on your own experience (particularly if you grew up in the church), isolate the congregations to which you have belonged, pinpoint the leadership, and analyze the consequences in terms of how well that church moved to action. Keep in mind what you have read in this chapter.

7

TEN COMMON BOTTLENECKS IN THE CHURCH (AND HOW TO DEAL WITH THEM)

As one analyzes churches, there seem to be ten recurring bottlenecks that hinder a church's effectiveness for discipleship. These bottlenecks occur in small and large churches of different denominations. They are roadblocks for declining churches and challenges for the ones that want to move to action.

Identifying them helps the members of your church realize that your congregation is not the only one that is faced with bottlenecks. The fact that bottlenecks are so common does not lessen their severity or importance, but it does help to see that these are ways that the devil tries to frustrate the people of God who want to grow up in faith, grow together in fellowship, reach out to others, and multiply churches around the world. As each is identified, it can be dealt with so that the church can be more effective.

PASTOR

The pastor as a necessary leader has already been discussed in the previous chapter. But how do you face the challenge of a pastor who is actually hindering the effectiveness of your church?

Most of all, love your pastor. It is a difficult job to be a pastor. No matter what the pastor thinks or does, there is a strong possibility that the pastor means well. Anyone who is willing to submit to the call of God to the pastoral ministry takes on the role of a servant and much hard work. The stress level is high. The pastor is on call twenty-four hours a day. There are pressures on the family. Since it is a public position, there is always someone who doesn't like the pastor.

Pray for your pastor. Each member of the church should pray for the pastor every day. This is part of what follower-ship is all about. Send your pastor a note. Let your pastor know that you are offering prayerful guidance.

If your pastor seems to be a bottleneck or a roadblock for your church, *talk to your pastor—not to others.* Never talk about your pastor in a negative way to others. Instead, sit down and talk one-on-one. Share with your pastor in a lov-ing way your concerns for the church. Pastors are easily susceptible to burnout. Make sure your church insists that your pastor gets rest. The pastor should get a day off each week and take vacations.

Pastors are liable to become stale. Your congregation should *sponsor an educational opportunity for your pastor* at least a week or two every year. Sometimes attending a sem-inar or workshop will help your pastor see the ministry at your church objectively, and then will begin to recognize that he has been a bottleneck to its vitality, health, and growth.

Use an outside consultant. It is inappropriate to bring in a consultant to manipulate your pastor out of position. Most consultants will have nothing to do with this. But many times a congregation will ask a consultant to conduct an analysis, and within that context the consultant will have an opportunity to discuss with the pastor personal strengths and weaknesses. If the pastor is a bottleneck, an outsider will see this and will deal with it without embar-rassing the pastor in front of the congregation.

As a Christian, *help your pastor reach full potential*—all that God has intended. Don't ever work against your pastor, for that doesn't honor Christ or his church. With the help of

loving members, many pastors who were formerly bottlenecks in the congregation have become driving forces for
Christ in a lifestyle of discipleship and mission.

PEOPLE

There will always be bottleneck people in your church.
Love them! Yet it is also your responsibility to challenge
them. In a spirit of love, help them catch the vision of your
church's mission. In a loving and ethical Christian way, try
to discourage negative people from having a decision-
making influence in the church. The fact that some disagree
does not make them negative people. It is when they
become disagreeable that they are negative. Every church
has a few disagreeable people. They need to be loved and
overwhelmed by the kindness of Christ. They also need to
be isolated from new Christians who may be infected by
their negativism. Not everyone will want to move forward
in discipleship and mission. There will never be 100 percent
of any congregation involved in moving the church forward in health and vitality. But it takes only a core group of
people to move a church. Many of those who have not yet
seen the vision will catch it later.

Try to evaluate people within their context. Think about
their point of view or perspective. Consider other aspects of
their lives that might help explain why they are negative.
Sometimes they have problems at home, at work, or at
school that spill over into their lives and their attitudes at
the church. Minister to their needs. Don't fight fire with fire.
Fight fire with water—the water of love. The key to transforming negative people into positive people is always
their spiritual growth. If you can accomplish only one
thing, help get them into the Word of God. Peter wrote that
"love covers over a multitude of sins" (1 Pet. 4:8). As we
love one another, we will be able to tolerate one another.

Patience is an important fruit of the Spirit when it comes to dealing with negative people. Don't ignore them. Challenge them. Sit down and listen to them; talk with them. If you can, pray together. The Spirit of God has a remarkable way of melting negativism through the power of prayer.

Money

There is enormous wealth among Christians in North America. In their bank accounts, these Christians have the power to finance just about anything. It is unfortunate that numerous ministries suffer so much simply because of a lack of money. People who give their lives for the service of the Kingdom have enough frustrations and challenges without the added concern of finances. Yet many Christian organizations, churches, and disciples involved in mission and ministry are burdened by financial challenges.

What a sad situation that money is a bottleneck! Some churches have large sums of money on deposit or invested. Other churches have endowment funds. Some churches own stocks and bonds. Although there is nothing wrong with having some "cushion" for a "rainy day," the church is not a bank. What an embarrassment it would be if the church found itself sitting on large sums of money when the Lord returns. It is especially sad that some churches and individuals sit on such enormous wealth when many ministries on the cutting edge of world evangelization are in such desperate need.

Nevertheless, money is not really the most important ingredient in a movement. It is essential because it is part of reality. The world operates on a money basis. But ideas are a much more powerful ingredient than money. Throughout history God has produced marvelous results through individuals, agencies, and churches that operated on shoestring budgets. Good ideas usually attract money, especially if the needs are publicized. Therein lies the challenge for the Christian church and world evangelization. Christians need to know the dramatic needs of those who are working so hard for the fulfillment of the Great Commission.

The problem is not a money problem but a giving problem. Ultimately, it is a spiritual problem that needs the application of God's Word.

Many church leaders are afraid to ask for money. Actually, there are more people willing to give than there are people willing to ask. James says, "You do not have, because you do not ask God" (4:2). Although that passage refers to asking God directly for what we need, I believe this also applies to asking God's people through whom God supplies needs.

Perhaps the greatest need lies in raising people, not raising money. When people see a vision for mission, when they see a genuine need, and when they understand the importance of reaching others for Christ, it will affect their giving.

One of the reasons congregations face financial challenges is that they have failed to realize how the world of wealth has changed in the last several decades. This is especially true in the Western world. With the development of Social Security, pension plans, health plans, bonuses, and stock options, people no longer accumulate wealth in just one way. The paycheck was once the sum and substance of wealth. That has changed. It has become only a part of people's assets. The fringe benefits are the other part.

When people give their weekly offering, they often give a percentage of their regular weekly income. But since this represents only a portion of their wealth, the overall percentage of giving is far less than it once was. This is what might be called "left-pocket wealth." But what about tapping the "right-pocket wealth"—those blessings from God that are accumulated through fringe benefits?

Generally, people tap right-pocket wealth for special

causes. When a church has a fund-raising campaign for a building, or a special support event for a missionary or mission agency, people tend to tap their right-pocket wealth. When people remember the church in their wills, this also enables them to give back to God a portion of their right-pocket wealth. Congregations need to help people recognize that the right-pocket wealth is a blessing from God that can in turn be a blessing for the work of Christ in this world.

One of the healthiest things a congregation can do is to support Christian ministry beyond its doors. God seems to bless congregations that resist the temptation of selfishness and give away a large portion of their tithes and offerings.

There are several areas beyond the congregation in which the church should participate and support God's work. A portion should be sent to the denomination. Denominations can accomplish certain ministries (like colleges, seminaries, and missionary activities) that congregations cannot provide individually. Further, many churches find great satisfaction in being involved in personalized missionary support. A church adopts a missionary family or a mission project and receives a direct report on how its money is being used and what it is accomplishing. Often the missionaries will visit the church to give a direct report when they are home on furlough. This is an excellent way of providing support and developing ownership for that support. It also stimulates the minds of people to the possibility of becoming missionaries themselves.

Another area of Christian work that is worthy of a congregation's support is found among the many independent, nonprofit agencies that God is raising up in the church. These are cutting-edge groups. They are usually led by a visionary person and are directed to a specific ministry to which the group feels called. They include agencies like Bible societies, evangelistic associations, youth ministries, Bible translators, and church-growth ministries. Often the

staff members live and work at great risk and personal sacrifice. Groups like these are historically known for accomplishing some of the greatest ministry for the expansion of
God's kingdom. The challenge to support them broadens
the vision of the congregational members to what God is
accomplishing through a variety of ministries.

Lifeless Worship

Many people first come into contact with the church and
the gospel of Jesus Christ in a corporate worship setting.
They are invited to church by a friend or neighbor, are
brought to worship by a relative, or simply visit a church on
their own. No matter how they come in, what they experience in that first worship service will have a great impact
on whether they will come back and whether they are able
to listen to the gospel message. The church has only one
chance to make a first impression. Visitors (and members!)
need to feel God's love. Worship, therefore, should be
uplifting and alive, relevant and meaningful.

People today want more than an intellectual approach to
worship. They have greater needs experientially. In other
words, worship needs to be an experience. People need to
"feel" the love of God, the expectations of the fulfillment of
God's promises, the celebration of God's forgiveness, and
the joy of new life with Christ, as it is expressed in the gra-
cious message of God to his people, received in a visible
way in the sacraments, and celebrated in the lives of the
people. This is not to say that worship should be mere
entertainment. But it can be joyful and meaningful. There is
nothing sinful in being happy in worship. Unfortunately, in
many worship services the members appear to have been
baptized in vinegar.

For worship to be meaningful, Christianity needs to be
more than an emphasis on correct teaching and how to get

to eternity. Worship needs to include application of the Scriptures to everyday life. Further, people need to hear from each other. They need to have a mechanism whereby they share with each other what God is doing in their lives. Worship and Bible study need to be considered as a unit, two sides of one experience.

Preaching today needs to go beyond the sixteenth-century model of the academic classroom setting. It is increasingly hard to communicate effectively through the lecture method to a generation that has grown up on *Sesame Street*. Concept-oriented people will respond more readily to parables, dialogue, visual aids, and drama. That is why in many churches the adults can be asked on the following Tuesday about the worship service, and they will remember the children's sermon but will have forgotten the message delivered from the pulpit.

The music needs to be in the heart language of the people. If the congregation is located in a German settlement, then the heart language of the people is German. They should sing German songs. If the people are traditional in their mind-set toward the world, the music should be traditional. If the people are Hispanic, the words should not only be in Spanish, but the music should be in the style and tempo of Hispanic music, using instruments that are reflective of that culture. If the church is serious about reaching African American people, the style and the rhythm of the music should be appealing to an African American population. If a church wants to reach Anglos who were born after World War II, it should recognize that they dance to the beat of a different drum.

Many Hispanics, African Americans, and post–World War II baby boomers have been enculturated to accept and appreciate ancient and traditional forms and styles of music. But if a church is concerned about reaching the unchurched people in these groups, the process will be slow and ineffective when the enculturation process is forced on them. It is far more effective for the salvation of people if they hear the gospel in their own heart language. Many churches today offer a variety of worship styles. This will be discussed in chapter 9.

UNCLEAR PURPOSE

Another common bottleneck is the lack of a clearly defined purpose. Although this was discussed in an earlier chapter, it is mentioned again here because it is a common bottleneck that must be removed.

The purpose of the church must penetrate every activity and organization within the church. Further, the congregation is obligated to tell people what the church stands for. It is essential to clarify to a potential member what the church members believe and practice. People today are looking for a church that really cares about what people believe. They need the Body of Christ with a backbone, where people know what they believe and are willing to stand by their convictions. In my book *Your Church Has Personality* (Lima, Ohio: Fairway Press, 1997), I have described the way in which a church can develop a philosophy-of-ministry statement to help communicate the unique aspects of the congregation. A church needs to keep communicating its vision and the direction in which it is moving.

Congregations must help leaders remain clear about the direction of the church. Unity among the leadership about the purpose of the church is essential for effective teamwork and for discipleship and mission.

The church should take inventory regularly to reflect on where the ministry has been and how it is proceeding. To do this effectively, there needs to be a clear benchmark of the purpose and direction.

Many churches are not clear about purpose. When that is the case, the church can drift aimlessly. God had a clear intent in sending Jesus Christ. Jesus had a crystal-clear picture of his mission. He intends for his Body to be clear about its direction, priorities, and mission.

COMMUNICATION INSIDE

Members of congregations need to hear regularly from their churches. Beyond the formal setting of a worship service, members need personal contact. Newsletters help, but the personal touch is important.

Some congregations train their leaders to visit in the homes of members for other reasons besides pledges for financial support. Especially in smaller churches and in some rural churches, there is a high expectation that the pastor will visit each home once a year or every few years. Even in larger churches, pastors should have some personal contact with members on a regular basis. In larger churches, pastors may be able to visit people in their homes only once every five years. In multiple-staff situations it may not always be the senior pastor who makes visits. Nevertheless, staff visits can do much to encourage people in their Christian lives and in the ownership of the congregation.

In churches with Christian day schools, teachers should visit the families of children in their classes at least twice, once before school starts and once during the school year. Sunday school teachers should visit in the homes of their students two or three times each year. These visits should be ministry visits, not just social visits. This means that beyond the friendly discussions and small talk about the weather, jobs, and sports, the caller should talk about the spiritual aspects of life, lead a short Bible study, and close in prayer.

The actionary church needs a system by which it is immediately known if a person is absent from church. Some churches have no system for keeping attendance records and rely on haphazard methods of recognizing that someone was absent. Other churches have a system, but evaluate attendance only on a quarterly basis. If people miss more than four weeks (of worship), they may be well on the way to becoming "hard-core" delinquents. It is very late at that point to respond with a call. It is more important for the congregation to have some form of shepherding system by which a person's absence from church is promptly detected and a follow-up call is made.

Incidentally, this is one of the first areas of church life to suffer when a church is understaffed. As a church grows, it requires a strong effort to continue to equip those involved in shepherding ministry to care for the members of the congregation.

Good communication within the church requires that various groups communicate with each other. Often in the Body of Christ, the right hand doesn't know what the left hand is doing. It is important to have formal, intentional communication systems so that this takes place.

One of the most important aspects of internal communication in a healthy and vital church is training and equipping people to talk *with* each other, not *against* each other. Gossip is one of the most hideous sins that Satan uses to divide and conquer the people of God. People need to learn the truths of Matthew 18 regarding approaching another person directly. Christians also need to be clear about the sin of slander. It would be hard to prove, but gossip probably destroys the Christian faith of thousands of people every year, because they become discouraged, hurt, and dismayed about the church.

When it is appropriate to criticize people in the church, it should be done in a Christian manner. We should use the apostle Paul's method of constructive criticism. Whenever Paul wanted to correct people, he always started with a list of positive things for which he thanked God. Then he expressed the concerns he had. As he finished his letter, he gave thanks and praise to God for the strengths of the people. Basically, his method was to surround criticism with love and genuine praise. This "sandwich" method still works twenty centuries later.

Another important aspect of communication within the church is encouragement of one another. There was a man in the New Testament named Joseph who was known for his encouraging ministry. He even acquired a nickname by which we know him today—Barnabas. The name "Barnabas" simply means "son of encouragement." Every Christian needs a good dose of the Barnabas style. What would your congregation be like if every person attending worship made it a point to encourage at least one other person everytime he or she came to church?

Building one another up in the Christian faith is an important part of the lifestyle of the Body of Christ. This is called edification. In the New Testament, the root word for edification comes from the task of mending a net. That's interesting, since the church is called a net (Matt. 13:47) and Christians are called to be "fishers of men" (Matt. 4:19).

In New Testament times, most of the fishing was done with nets. Think about that concept. If the church has people who are weak, hurting, and in need of encouragement, the net must be full of holes. It is a church that needs mending. As people build one another up, they are involved in mending the net. And when a congregation has a strong net, it catches fish. As a group of fishers for people, the congregation is much stronger in attracting and keeping new people in the fellowship when it is characterized by a solid ministry of encouragement.

Many researchers have conducted studies among relatively new members of a church. The people were asked why they decided to stay at the church that they eventually joined. For the last two decades many people have responded with the same answers: They stay because

(1) there is a relevant message and (2) the people are friendly. That is edification at work.

Communication Outside

One bottleneck that keeps many churches from moving to action is the way people represent their church outside the Christian family. In talking to others, people must speak well of their church. It is essential that members of the church keep "dirty laundry" from public view. That is not being untruthful with the people of the community. It is simply keeping family business inside the family. The problem with sharing the church's difficulties with people outside is that people outside the church don't know the positive side of life at the church, the dynamics of forgiveness, and the surpassing greatness of knowing Christ Jesus. The negative message could discourage them from ever attending a church. That means that they may never hear the gospel. Hearing about the problems within the church could be a roadblock keeping a person from the good news of eternal life. Share the message of Jesus instead. Keep other concerns in their proper place.

Churches need to be aggressive about telling their community who they are and what they believe. It is amazing how many people in a community know little about the churches in their area. Sometimes what they do know is inaccurate and discourages them from attending. Churches should communicate regularly and in a variety of ways. (This will be discussed in more detail in chapter 9.)

Many churches would greatly improve their communication to their community by changing the sign in front of the church. Most churches have a sign that is too small for drivers who pass by to read. Further, most church signs are parallel to the road rather than perpendicular. Most business signs are perpendicular, so it seems odd that many churches have failed to notice this and have placed their signs parallel to the road. A readable, perpendicular sign would greatly enhance the communication of the church's message.

My favorite church sign is at a church in Kentucky where I served as a consultant. The only sign anywhere near the building was a street sign that read "Dead End." There was more meaning to that sign than either the church or the street department ever intended.

Communication with the community can be enhanced by direct mail. Churches can use direct mail to reach the people in their ministry areas several times a year. Telephone ministry is becoming popular, as congregations are involved in training people to contact the unchurched in the community.

By far, the best communication to the community is through people who know people in the congregation. When church members are equipped to share their faith at the right time and in the right way with those they know, it is far more effective than when unchurched people are contacted by strangers. That is why lifestyle evangelism programs like *Heart to Heart* (Corunna, Ind.: Church Growth Center, 1995), written by Steve Wagner, are popular; churches use them to equip people to share their faith with people they know and with whom they already feel comfortable.

When communicating with the community, many churches tend to "broadcast." Broadcasting is important. For example, it is important to send a mailing to all the people in the ministry area. But "narrowcasting" is also a vital strategy for communication. Narrowcasting is meeting the specific needs and talking the language of a specific group. For instance, if a church discovers that there are many young children in its community, it may decide to start a preschool, a day-care center, or a "mother's morning out" program. The broadcast method would advertise such ministries by placing a sign in front of the church or putting an ad in one of the local newspapers. A narrowcasting method would develop a ministry in which members would clip birth announcements out of the paper. They could then send the new parents a card, and within a couple of years begin sending them information about the church's ministries for parents of young children.

There are many ways in which narrowcasting can be used to meet the felt needs of the community and to develop bridges for sharing the gospel as the congregation moves out in mission to the people in its ministry area.

Negativism

Negative people can have a tremendous influence on a church. They can discourage others and help develop a dark cloud over the church. Unfortunately, these people rarely know the effects of their negativism. Sometimes it is simply an expression of their lifestyles, as they reflect in the church the way they react to everything.

There seem to be some people in every church who are just plain contrary. If you say "black," they say "white." If you say "day," they say "night." I have a son who went through what people call the "terrible twos." One of his favorite responses was the word *no*. Perhaps some of the negative people in the church never grew out of the terrible twos. Their negativism dampens the spirits of others who want to work and serve the Lord, causes weaker Christians to feel bad about their church, and has a tremendous negative impact on the congregation's finances. Negativism can be a serious bottleneck for the church that wants to move to action.

For some reason, unfortunately, few people sit down and discuss this problem—in love—with the negative people. Perhaps they fear that the negative person will begin to speak badly about them, but that is one of the risks of Christianity. These people need to know in a loving and kind way (using the apostle Paul's "sandwich" style of correction) that they are having a bad effect on others' lives.

Some pastors are the source of negativism in the church. Occasionally, sermons sound negative, speaking primarily to the people who are not present. When a pastor begins to have negative-sounding sermons, it is sometimes an indication of burnout. A subtle change in the tone of the sermons may be a sign that your pastor needs help. Listen carefully the next time your pastor returns from a vacation, and analyze the sermon for the positive aspects. Pastoral burnout may be a sign that your church is understaffed.

People can receive enough negative communication at home by reading the newspaper and watching television. They don't need to come to church to hear it. People need to leave church feeling positive about God's love in Jesus Christ, about themselves, about other Christians, and about the church. That does not mean that the Law should not be preached, just that it must be carefully distinguished from the gospel. The gospel should always predominate. Focusing on Jesus allows the Spirit to produce positive results (Rom. 8:5-8).

Unwillingness to Change

These words are often quoted as the last seven words of the church: "We've never done it that way before." Resistance to change was the mark of the Pharisees at the time of the ministry of Jesus Christ. It is also a problem and a great bottleneck in the church today.

It is human nature for us to become comfortable doing things the way that we have always done them. When the church is planted on new soil, change is easy. But tradition sets in the next day. After many years, the church becomes irrelevant and begins to decline.

Resistance to change is one of the many reasons why the church declines. The church flourished in the Mediterranean world of the New Testament. Then it moved to Europe, and the church around the Mediterranean languished. As the church moved to the New World, the American church prospered while the European church dwindled. Today, the church is growing with enthusiasm and excitement around the Pacific Rim countries: China, Indonesia, the Philippines, and South Korea. Will the church decline on the North American continent? It will if God's people remain resistant to change.

The gospel never changes. The Bible is the Bible, and God's Word always remains. What God did for us in sending his Son is finished, sealed, and unalterable. The church must remain immovable in its teaching, while in its packaging, communication, music, building, and style it is always flexible.

Cultural Baggage

It is often hard for Christians to discern where the pure teaching of God's Word ends and culture begins. Wherever we travel, our cultural baggage goes with us.

It is especially hard for a church to react appropriately when a new cultural group moves into its neighborhood. I remember the women's group of an old Anglo church that found itself in a young African American community. The women (bless their hearts) began to have a vision for mission. They saw an opportunity to reach people in their community. They decided to have a community supper and offer it free of charge to anyone. Their intentions were good, but they could not unpack their cultural baggage. They served knockwurst and sauerkraut!

Every group in a society has its own culture. Sometimes that culture is similar enough for an existing church to reach a particular group. But sometimes it is necessary to reach people by speaking a different language, offering different food, and singing different songs. The cultural baggage bottleneck, particularly acute for churches in changing communities, can be overcome only by starting in-culture churches (churches targeted to a specific culture). Because society is made up of different cultural groups, there is a great need for thousands more churches in every land, and in every culture. Every person on earth has a right to hear the gospel in his or her own language and in the style of his or her culture.

Paul's strategy for not putting roadblocks in front of anyone can be examined in Romans 14–15 and 1 Corinthians 8. His approach is summarized in these words: "Each of us should please his neighbor for his own good, to build him up. For even Christ did not please himself but, as it is written: 'The insults of those who insult you have fallen on me'" (Rom. 15:2-3).

These are the ten most common bottlenecks for churches that want to move to action for discipleship and mission. It is most important to be sensitive to God's will for his church. By the power of God's Spirit, a church can deal with bottlenecks as challenges, be victorious, and let God's gospel pour out freely to the ends of the earth.

Discussion Questions

1. Identify the bottlenecks in your church. Develop strategies to overcome them.

2. Do any of your bottlenecks differ from the ten discussed? Are they unique to your church, common elsewhere, or perhaps only sub-bottlenecks of the ten?

3. How does your church demand competence and growth in your pastor? Consider time available for family, compulsory days off, educational or refresher opportunities, community and denominational involvement,

relief in preaching and other tasks (particularly attendance at meetings), love, concern, and prayer.

4. Every church has negative people. What causes negativism? What new ministries will you establish to channel this misspent energy into something positive that serves the Lord?

5. How can you implement a study of spiritual gifts to guide all members into searching for that part of the Body of Christ where each has been called to be?

6. Appoint a task force to determine what spiritual gifts are appropriate to each office, role, committee, organization, ministry, and task in your church.

8

HONORING YOUR CONTEXT

Dealing with bottlenecks within a congregation is an important task, but there is another essential part of the mix for moving a church to action: analyzing and understanding the church's context—its community.

Two general principles apply to churches within the context of their communities. First, most pastors and church leaders underestimate the influence that the national and local contexts have on the church, and they can do nothing about it. Second, most pastors and church leaders overestimate the degree to which the community is aware of the church.

The impact of the immediate area around the church is substantial. Its influence often is not taken into consideration when leaders are trying to understand the church's vitality and growth. For example, several years ago congregations in many communities recorded lower numbers of children enrolled in Sunday school. Some concerned church leaders blamed the Sunday school teachers, while others criticized the curriculum. Still others shrugged their shoulders and blamed apathetic parents. But at least part of the reason for the trend was the lower birthrates in many communities over the previous years, which meant that fewer children were available as prospects for Sunday school.

Another example of how a congregation can be affected by its community is reflected in the story of Bethel Church, which is located in a suburb of metropolitan Detroit. Due to tremendous growth in the community, the main road was being widened. The highway department condemned the front third of the sanctuary. This was a devastating event for some of the members. But with proper consultation and direction, the congregation was led to see it as a great blessing. It resulted in the long overdue demolition of the outmoded facilities and brought about the construction of a new worship center. This brought new life and vitality to the congregation.

The third illustration of the serious effect that context can have on a church is the story of Faith Church, a congregation located in Philadelphia. Faith was an economically solid, healthy African American congregation of upwardly mobile middle-management people who found themselves in the midst of a changing neighborhood. African Americans of a lower socioeconomic level were moving into the area around the church. Many of the members of the congregation were moving to an economically more expensive African American community a few miles away and commuting to the church. The new group around the church had a different lifestyle, economic level, and educational background. The two groups didn't have much in common, and even though the neighborhood remained mostly African American, the change from one economic group to another caused Faith Church to become an island of one kind of people in a sea of another.

Sometimes the context helps to clarify why certain trends take place in the church. For example, just about every pastor has sat in the office after a worship service and tried to figure out why the attendance suddenly dropped that Sunday. All sorts of doubts run through a pastor's mind at a time like that. "Did I say something wrong? Am I losing my quality of preaching? Are people boycotting the church for some reason?"

At times like these, pastors and church leaders need to honor the context and make a few phone calls to other pastors in the immediate area. More often than not, if the trend is sudden and dramatic, phone calls will reveal that other churches have experienced the same trend. A quick call to the local school superintendent's office may show that absenteeism has risen over the last couple of weeks. Contact with a local physician may indicate that the number of cases of flu or colds has risen dramatically. Much wasted energy and many false conclusions and incorrect perceptions spring from an unwillingness to honor the immediate context.

There is also the greater context that includes national and world trends. These too affect the local congregation. For example, are people today more or less religious than they used to be?

Some people, noting the decline in membership and attendance in mainline denominations, would conclude that people are less religious today. But there is much evidence to the contrary. Many newer denominations and numerous independent churches are growing rapidly. Further, within every declining denomination there are glaring exceptions of congregations that are growing dramatically. In addition, interest in the occult and sects is strong. Supernatural themes in books, plays, movies, and songs reflect that, however misguided their search may be, many people are thinking and wondering about life in the spiritual dimension. In the Christian world, contemporary Christian music has been a growing enterprise. Many of the youth who listen to Christian music attend concerts and are involved in high school and college Christian youth organizations. They may not be involved in traditional churches on Sunday, but they are active Christians.

When studying the general context of a society or a denomination, it is helpful to ask which churches are growing and why, and which churches are declining and why. One of the most helpful ways to understand the religious trends of society is to visit growing churches.

Is one of the reasons that certain churches are growing related to their doctrinal stance? Only insofar as the congregation fully supports a doctrinal commitment to evangelism, outreach, and meeting people's needs.

Church attendance trends are also affected by influences found in whole societies. For example, research shows that when national challenges are faced, people often respond by attending church more often. This is especially true when a serious military conflict occurs, as it did during the Gulf War. In the mid-1980s, church attendance jumped after "Black Monday," the day the stock market fell drastically. There is a national mood of the people. As they feel comfortable and safe, many people relax their religious fervor, and church attendance goes down. Human nature being what it is, when there is a crisis, church attendance rises. This has led some church leaders to say with a prophetic-sounding voice, "What the country needs now is a serious plague or famine." While no Christian would wish a crisis of pain or death, it is important for Christians to be ready to respond in a time of need. The Oklahoma City bombing was a nightmare event for Americans. Yet, few churches even addressed the issue of national grief being felt by the masses. Any wonder people feel that the church is irrelevant.

National trends seem to have a dramatic effect on behavior in the church. Even though the effect may be subconscious, these trends do change people's behavior. Likewise, periods of affluence tend to affect church attendance in a negative way. When people have more discretionary money to spend, they often travel and vacation to a greater degree, and worship attendance declines.

Similarly, the weather can have an enormous impact. Not long ago a large and severe snowstorm hit the middle of Canada and the United States. Worship services in ten states and three provinces were canceled in most churches on Christmas Eve and Christmas Day. Snowstorms in most of these places hit consecutively on three of the following Saturday evenings. For many of these churches, this was the first time in recorded history that such severe weather had occurred with such devastating timing. Although there was some financial recuperation due to loyal members who brought in their offerings after the weather cleared in late January, those who did not make up their contributions caused losses of millions of dollars for the churches of those states and provinces. The result was deficit spending and financial difficulties that continued in some of those churches for more than two years. It took some time before they were able to regain the financial momentum lost during the storms. In a domino effect, the amount these churches gave to the denominational headquarters was reduced and had an effect on entire church bodies.

WHAT ARE THE UNCHURCHED THINKING?

For actionary congregations that want to understand their mission context and reach the unchurched, it is expedient to know what unchurched people are thinking. That will make it possible to build appropriate and relevant strategies for reaching them with the gospel.

For example, people on the North American continent were once open to confrontation. This was especially true in the 1960s and early 1970s, when confrontations on college campuses and in labor disputes were common. During this time, confrontational methods of evangelism worked well. Callers from churches knocked on doors and addressed people with challenging questions about their understanding of eternal life. That method still works well with many people. But there is a growing number of unchurched people with whom that strategy will not work. People today, including many who are unchurched, are more relation oriented. Consequently, lifestyle evangelism strategies appear to be gaining in popularity because they are effective in reaching these people.

Unfortunately, many Christians are not in tune with what unchurched people are thinking. Most Christians associate only with other church people. Therefore, it takes an extra effort on the part of the church to discover what the unchurched are thinking.

There are two primary strategies for discovering what is on the minds of unchurched people. First, every church should survey its immediate area for at least one year. This survey should be conducted among a random sampling of homes, asking questions that relate to people's religious views. When these surveys are designed to measure church attendance, it's easy to isolate people who are unchurched. This is usually a great learning experience for Christians and helps them keep their worldview sensitive to those who are outside the church.

A second strategy for understanding the unchurched is to interview visitors to the church. It is also important to talk to new members as they become assimilated into the church. Both visitors and new members can share a wealth of information about what attracted them to the church and what needs they have that the church is meeting. Many assimilation programs give new members a lot of information about the church, but fail to make an effort to hear from them. The church that honors its context and has a vision for reaching unchurched people will listen to what the new members have to say.

One of the best handbooks on what unchurched people are thinking is *TV Guide*. Even the advertisements in the magazine reveal a slice of life beyond the walls of the church. Television is a powerful indicator of what people are thinking. Every pastor should know which shows are the most popular at any given time.

It is almost impossible to preach a relevant sermon if a

pastor hasn't seen at least one episode of each of the most popular shows on television, whether the pastor likes them or not. This applies also to films that are box-office hits and books on the best-seller list.

The four or five authors who are continually on the best-seller list of Christian books have become sensitive to Christian and semi-churched people. These key authors are not just good writers; they are also aware of people and their needs. Every pastor and key church leader needs to be familiar with these authors and what they are writing. Even if they don't agree with what the writers say, they ought to know what the people in their church are reading.

OPENNESS: WINDOWS OF OPPORTUNITY

There are at least seven important occasions when people will be more open to Christians who desire to share the love of God and the good news of Jesus Christ with them:

1. *When people move into a community, they tend to be open to new things.* They are making new friends and shopping in new stores. Their children are attending new schools. For several months they are open to an invitation to a church, even if they were unchurched in their former community.

Organizations like Welcome Wagon, which visits newcomers in the community, are aware of this receptivity. Many organizations and businesses use Welcome Wagon as a means of giving free coupons or discounts to people when they move into the community, because they know that people are developing new habits and lifestyles. Consequently, it is important for the church to extend an invitation to these people soon after they move into an area rather than waiting until their lifestyles are more established.

2. *When people are changing jobs or making career moves, whether they change residences or not, they are more open to*

change. Consequently, they are more open to an invitation to church or a meaningful presentation of the gospel. Many people today are changing careers during their late twenties and again during their "midlife crisis." It is becoming much more fashionable for a person to switch careers halfway through life. During this time of change, there is a window of opportunity for people to be more open to Christianity and the church. If Christians are trained to be sensitive to this, they will be on the lookout for new employees at their workplace and invite them to church.

3. *People who have visited the church are more open than people who have not visited.* If evangelism teams or leaders of the church visit these people in their homes, the teams or leaders are much more likely to be welcomed when they identify that they are from the church that the people just visited. Many rapidly growing churches make it a point to visit the people the afternoon of the people's first visit. Other churches try to visit within forty-eight hours.

4. *Those who have been helped by the church are more open to an invitation or a presentation of the good news of Jesus Christ.* For example, if a family has experienced the loss of its home by fire, and the congregation provides them with temporary housing, clothes, and goods, the family is much more likely to be open to the congregation. Helping people in itself is not evangelism (according to the discipleship model of the Scriptures), but it is indeed a way in which God often builds a bridge to the hearts of those who come to know the Savior.

5. *People who are friends of new members are often more receptive to the church.* For example, when Bob and Evelyn first joined the church, they were enthusiastic about their new life in Christ and their new association with God's people. Their enthusiasm spilled over to their friends, relatives, neighbors, and other acquaintances. Many of those friends were unchurched, but they were curious about the new excitement and the positive attitudes reflected by Bob and

Evelyn. When Bob and Evelyn were officially brought into the church, there was a special worship service. The congregation provided engraved invitations for Bob and Evelyn to share with all their friends. Many of their friends responded to the invitation and attended the service. Those who were unchurched became more open to the possibility of joining Bob and Evelyn in their new adventure of faith.

6. *Economic difficulties tend to create an openness in people.* Human nature is such that people tend to become self-reliant. When things are going well, some people forget about the need for the Christian faith. But when economic difficulties strike, people are reminded of the frailty of life. (This is also true at the time of a sudden death, a divorce, or the birth of a child.)

7. *Basic changes in society, or milestones in history, are also times when people are often more open to Christianity.* Many Christians believe, now that the twenty-first century has begun, that people will be more receptive to Christ and the church. Furthermore, many evangelism and mission strategists are targeting the next few years as a goal for world evangelization and the fulfillment of the Great Commission. Therefore in this new century there will be great mission activity. As people are reminded about the passing of time, they are also challenged to think about their own mortality, and often become more open to the good news of eternal life through Jesus Christ.

God's Rainbow of People Groups

As you seek to understand the context for your church, it is important to recognize the complexity of your community. The "people group" method provides a useful way for looking at the world.

How does God see the world? Human beings tend to look at the world in units of miles or kilometers, or they see geopolitical entities—counties, states, provinces, cities, or towns. But based on several Scripture passages, many biblical scholars and mission strategists believe that God speaks of the world in terms of people groups. People groups are defined in many ways in the Bible: tribes, languages, nations, and races. When a congregation sees its community as a mosaic of people groups, it is much more likely to develop a special evangelistic strategy for each group. Instead of looking at a town or area and considering all the people to be the same, the church becomes sensitive to the fact that not all the people are alike. Some may respond to the gospel in a different way from others.

Ten factors determine a people group:

1. *Race is sometimes a determinant for a people group, but it is not likely to be the dominant factor.*

2. *Language is a significant factor in defining a people group.* Greatly different languages are the easiest to detect and most visible group factors. What is more difficult to determine are slight differences in languages, like a southern drawl or northern black English.

3. *Lifestyle often delineates a people group.* The lifestyle of a particular group of people (campers, for example) may suggest that they would be unlikely candidates to attend church on a Sunday morning. Their schedule would require an evangelistic strategy that would invite them to church on a weeknight. Likewise, those who live in apartment complexes are often more responsive to a Bible study worship service held within the complex, at least initially.

4. *The economic level of a group may determine whether it is a people group.* In many modern societies this is one of the strongest factors of group identity.

5. *Educational level is also a strong determining factor for a people group.* Education often determines vocations and economic levels as well. All of these reflect lifestyle. Occasionally, education itself is a determining factor.

6. *Food sometimes helps identify a particular people group.* One

only has to think of certain foods, and immediately particular culture groups come to mind: blackened fish and seafood
gumbo, barbecued ribs and black-eyed peas, spaghetti and
lasagna, knockwurst and sauerkraut, burritos and fajitas.

7. *Unusual styles of dress are sometimes a distinguishing fea-
ture of a people group.* For example, it is common for young
African American men of a certain people group in New
York City to wear a hat indoors. This is part of the style of
the people group and has nothing to do with disrespect—
even as they wear the hats in church. Some Mennonite
women wear bonnets. Amish people wear very plain
clothes. Orthodox Jewish men wear skullcaps. Some people
are identified by designer blue jeans.

8. *Music can also illustrate the uniqueness of a people group.*
Various styles of music include classical, soul, hard rock,
country western, and many others.

9. *Occupation can define a people group.* People who work in
agriculturally oriented occupations, for example, often
reflect the worldview of a special people group. Their occupation has a great effect on their lifestyle. This is also true of
cab drivers, physicians, circus performers, college professors, politicians, and many others.

10. *Worldview is sometimes a determining factor for a people
group.* Yuppies, for example, have a way of looking at the
world that is much different from truck drivers, disc jock-
eys, racetrack employees, and Roman Catholic nuns.

Determining people groups is helpful when a church
wants to develop strategies for outreach so that it can touch
each segment of society in its community with the gospel of
Jesus Christ in a relevant way. This is one of the important
components of the mix that moves your church to action.

Discussion Questions

1. What do you really know about your community or
your church's area of ministry? Have you ever defined,

geographically or otherwise, those people for whom you feel directly and particularly responsible? List the main characteristics of the people around you.

2. Is your community changing? Is the makeup of your church body changing? Describe any changes or trends that have occurred within the last ten years, and analyze whether you have made changes in the ministry to meet or counter change.

3. How do you discover the needs of your community? List possible means of doing so. Develop strategies to implement several of these.

4. Of the seven "windows of opportunity" mentioned in this chapter, which are more appropriate for your area of ministry? How will you respond better?

5. Write a paragraph describing each of the dominant people groups in your church. What ministries respond to each of them? Are there emerging people groups for whom you must devise new ministries?

9

THE BASKIN-ROBBINS CHURCH

When the church recognizes God's rainbow of people groups, it becomes open to many strategies and opportunities for mission and ministry. This has many implications that are important components of the mix that moves the church to action.

The people-group approach to understanding the world helps the Christian church to distinguish the difference between raw Christianity and cultural packaging. For instance, I grew up in a Missouri Synod Lutheran church in the United States. When I thought about Lutherans, I thought of certain liturgies and styles of worship. The church of my youth was large. Therefore I thought in terms of large choirs, a big pipe organ, and lots of people. When I was young, this was my worldview of Christianity and of Lutheranism.

As I grew older and traveled, I began to see differences not only in Christianity but also among Lutherans. One of the greatest horizon-stretching experiences for me was to live in Australia for fourteen months. While we were there, my wife and I belonged to the Lutheran Church of Australia, which was fairly close in confessional beliefs to the Lutheran Church–Missouri Synod.

Then we made the thousand-mile trip to the center of the "outback." There in the middle of one of the largest deserts in the world is a Lutheran ministry to the Australian Aborigines. The mission was established more than a hundred years ago. We stayed at the mission for more than a week and had the opportunity to attend worship services with the Aborigines. It was a Lutheran church and a Lutheran worship service, but oh how different it was from the church back home. It was even vastly different from the other churches of the Lutheran Church of Australia to which we had grown accustomed. The Aborigines had a different style of music. The service was in a language we did not understand. Many of the components of worship were much different from what was familiar to us. Yet these people were as truly Lutheran as we were, or as Lutheran as Martin Luther himself, for that matter. They believed in the same Christ and subscribed to the same confessional writings that we did. But what a difference!

The beauty of Christianity is that it is transcultural. That means that it is above culture and can fit into any culture. Christianity does not condone a culture's habits when they are contrary to Scripture. But with regard to all the non-essentials, true and valid Christianity can fit various forms and styles. The good news can come in many packages, but the basic beliefs will be the same. That's why Lutherans in some parts of the world go to church wearing suits and ties, while Lutherans in other areas of the world wear loincloths. Some Lutherans listen to the music of a pipe organ played in a formal setting. Lutherans in other cultures dance to the beat of drums and tambourines. Of course this is also true of cultural expressions within Presbyterian, Baptist, Methodist, Roman Catholic, and other denominational families.

Christianity is a confident trust in Jesus Christ. It is not a matter of how you dress, what you eat, or what kind of music you like. It is not a certain way of talk, a certain style of worship, a particular type of building, or an ingrained set of traditions. This is a major issue for the effectiveness of the Christian church. It is an issue that is important not only for the church in the vastly different cultures that are found in other lands, but also for the church that has cultural differences within the same country, even within the same neighborhood.

This is not a new issue for the Christian church. The first challenge that the church faced in this regard is recorded in Acts 15. The apostle Paul had been sharing the gospel with Gentiles—those who were from a non-Jewish background. The Gentiles did not share the same traditions as the Jews. They didn't live according to the dietary laws and the other rules and regulations that were a part of life for practicing Jews. But the Gentiles were receptive to the gospel. Through Paul's preaching of the Word, the Holy Spirit penetrated their hearts, and many became Christians. When word of this reached Jerusalem, it upset a group of people known as the Judaizers. They were confused about the essentials of Christianity. Their argument was that if the Gentiles were going to become Christians, they had to follow the same traditions as the Jews. This meant that Gentile men would have to be circumcised. But Paul recognized that this demand was an attack on the gospel promise of Jesus Christ. He knew that being a child of God was defined by a confident dependence on God's grace in Jesus Christ, and nothing else. Its essence was an internal faith, not external signs.

And so that debate began. The church leaders met at Jerusalem and made a historic decision for Christianity. They decided that a Gentile could be a valid, 100 percent Christian without being circumcised and without following the rest of the traditional Jewish laws and cultural forms. This was a momentous decision, since it allowed Christianity to grow from a local sect to a world religion.

Even though it is clearly articulated in the Scriptures, many Christians today violate the principle that Christianity is above culture. I remember seeing a film many years ago that promoted the missionary activities of a large denomination in various countries in Africa. I remember clearly the scene in which several Africans, dressed in their limited native garb, were worshiping under the leadership of the missionary, who was roasting in the heat of the African sun. He was dressed in a liturgical vestment that had been exported from sixteenth-century Europe to seventeenth-century America and back across the ocean to twentieth-century Africa. In sixteenth-century Europe the vestment had symbolic meaning. In seventeenth-century America it expressed a tradition. In twentieth-century Africa it was a joke. A positive example of Christian sensitivity to people groups is the modern Jews for Jesus movement. After the first century, the Christian church became predominately a Gentile church. From that point on it was never very effective in reaching Jews. A change in culture similar to what the Judaizers had demanded of the Gentiles in the first century was generally required of the Jews by most Gentile Christians for the following nineteen centuries.

In the last several decades there has been an active effort to reach Jews for Jesus, the Messiah. They refer to Jesus as the "Messiah" rather than "Christ" because "Christ" (even though it means "Messiah") is a Gentile word.

Messianic Jews—as they are called—meet in Messianic synagogues, not churches. This is because the church, in the mind of the Orthodox Jew, is a Gentile organization. In the biblical sense, the Messianic synagogue is a church—the body of Christ—in every respect. The Messianic synagogue often does not have a "pastor," which may be considered a Gentile term. It has a rabbi in the office of the public ministry, who is essentially the same as a pastor in a Gentile church. When Messianic Jews go to the Lord's Supper, they receive the body and blood of Jesus the Messiah for the forgiveness of sins. They will often observe the Seder meal at the beginning of the Lord's Supper.

This strategy to reach Jews has been a major breakthrough for Jewish evangelism because it reaches them within their culture. Previously, a Jew who joined a Christian church would certainly be ostracized from family and friends. Now some Jews who become Christians in the religious sense remain Jews in many cultural externals, such as observing some of the Old Testament festivals or traditional national festivals; and observing practices like circumcision, the Sabbath meal in preparation for the Sabbath or even worshiping on the Sabbath (Saturday), and lighting the Sabbath candles.

This principle is extremely important for the local congregation. In any community, there are groups of people who are not against Jesus Christ but who need to hear about him in their own heart language and in their own cultural expression. This is especially true of churches in metropolitan areas where there is a large multicultural population.

What About Unity?

The Christian church has often confused unity with conformity. This confusion is boldly expressed in many ways in modern society. One indication of this confusion is the lack of clarity between "religion" and "denomination." For example, many hospitals have a question about religion on their admittance forms. They want to know what religion the patient professes. If the patient indicates "Christianity," it causes confusion because what the hospital really wants to know is the denominational preference.

The Bible talks about unity within the Christian church, not conformity in external matters. Paul speaks of "one body and one Spirit . . . one Lord, one faith, one baptism; one God and Father of all . . ." (Eph. 4:4-6). On this level there really is neither Jew nor Greek, slave nor free, white nor black, Hispanic nor Chinese. For those of us who have worshiped with people of vastly different cultures, like the

Aborigines, there is a wonderful beauty about being one in the Christian faith even though we are different in many other ways.

The Bible does not talk about conformity. The Bible talks about diversity, even within the Christian church. The New Testament speaks about the variety of gifts. The gifts are not the same; people are different. At the same time, people are unified in the family of Jesus Christ as brothers and sisters in the faith.

Individual denominations have a certain unity and uniqueness because of their confessional agreements on how the Scriptures are interpreted and understood. These agreements in teaching form the basis of a denomination's unity. But this unity is not to be confused with conformity. For a denomination to adhere to certain confessional standards of doctrine is one thing, but to demand the same language and music or even to publish an "official" hymnbook is a matter of conformity, not unity.

When unity is viewed as conformity in style, a church tends to provide ministry and outreach as if all the people in the community were the same. This is reflected in several ways.

1. *Worship services are only provided on Sunday, as if there were no firefighters, police, or nurses in the community.* These people often have to work on Sunday and need alternative opportunities for worship.

2. *Congregations provide only one kind of worship service.* This ignores the fact that some people in just about every community respond to formal worship, while others respond to less formal worship.

3. *Some churches provide only one kind of outreach program.* This does not take into account the fact that some people will respond to an invitation to church, while others will need to be reached in their homes. Still others don't want people coming to the door, but might be attracted to the church that helps them through drug abuse, alcoholism, or divorce.

4. *Some congregations have only one way to advertise their*

church, namely, a church sign. This assumes that everyone in town drives by the church or that everyone who drives by the church reads the sign.

We live in a Baskin-Robbins world. Baskin-Robbins is an ice-cream store that offers thirty-one flavors. It is all ice cream, to be sure. That is the essential characteristic of Baskin-Robbins. But the variety of flavors offered illustrates a clear understanding that people who like ice cream respond in different ways.

Too often the church tries to fit all people into one style of programming, worship life, and language. It's like fitting round pegs into square holes. Those who do not respond to the style are judged to be "resistant," not open to the gospel. But perhaps they never hear the gospel because it is not presented in a language, style, and form that they can understand.

CLASSICAL ONE-CHOICE THINKING

Many churches create roadblocks to the gospel because they don't have Baskin-Robbins thinking. For example, some churches offer just one women's group that meets during the middle of the day and provides no baby-sitting. Then they wonder why working women and young mothers don't care to join.

Another common way churches demonstrate a lack of Baskin-Robbins thinking is that in adding a second worship service, they offer it on the same day of the week (usually Sunday), at the same general time of the day (morning), and in the same general worship style. This may save the cost of printing different bulletins, but it is a glaring example of denying the multiplicity of people groups in the community. There are few communities in which a different style of worship service couldn't reach another segment of the community that is unchurched.

Another common way in which congregations reflect one-choice thinking is in how they offer a youth service. The idea of providing a youth-oriented service is a step in the right direction. But many churches follow a strategy that is detrimental. The bulletin reads: "On the fourth Sunday of the month, the second service will be a youth service. We are announcing this in advance, so those who want to attend the youth service will be sure to come to that service."

This strategy has serious problems. In the first place, it probably reveals a subtle attitude that the youth have to be pacified once in a while rather than acknowledging that a new generation of people can be an emerging people group. Second, it carries an understanding that when these youth get older, they will come to see what real worship is all about. It denies that language and music change, and that therefore the style of worship must change. It is the chauvinistic viewpoint of an older generation planting the seed of traditionalism that will almost guarantee the church's stagnation in several generations to come. Further, such a strategy programs some people to come to church once a month, and it encourages others to stay away from church at least once a month.

If a church is really serious about reaching a new generation for Christ, it should start another worship service at another time. This strategy basically plants a new congregation within the church. The new service should always be held at the same time every week, and the style should be consistent.

Another mistake of one-choice thinking is "blended worship," in which the traditional service is sprinkled with contemporary expressions. This guarantees that just about everyone will be uncomfortable at least once during the worship service.

A new worship experience (or any other new style of worship) should be tried for a minimum of eighteen months. Unfortunately, many churches try new worship services for a summer and then reevaluate.

One-choice thinking is also reflected in congregations that offer only one group Bible study opportunity—on Sunday morning. In smaller churches this may be necessary, but in larger congregations people require several opportunities for Bible study—on Sunday morning and at other times during the week as well. Recognizing the Baskin-Robbins approach to life, some of these studies need to be formal, some informal. Some need to be at church; others should be in homes. One of the best ways to reach businesspeople in the Western world is to provide a 6:00 A.M. breakfast Bible study at a restaurant.

One final illustration of a dramatic way in which churches are caught in one-choice thinking is that many of them think in terms of only one location. This mind-set of many Christians is such that they see their church growing larger and larger in the same place. But recognizing the need for many choices, churches would do well to be involved in church-planting activities in which they start new congregations that are not only geographically different but may also include a different style of worship and ministry.

TELLING YOUR CHURCH'S STORY

Good advertisers recognize that in a Baskin-Robbins world, people need to hear the story of their "product" in several different ways. Consequently, they use multiple methods of advertisement.

Coca-Cola, McDonald's, Pepsi, and Budweiser are good examples of companies that use multiple methods of advertising their products. For example, several months ago I heard a Budweiser beer commercial on my car radio. I noticed that they had a new theme. Over the next several days I noticed that they did not play that commercial just once, nor did it air on only one station. They were using multiple methods of advertising even though one medium. The next week I was watching television and saw the commercial with the same new theme. The next day I was looking through *Time* magazine, and I saw the advertisement again. A week later I was driving in another state, and I saw the same theme on a billboard. Budweiser is serious about getting its product into the hands of people.

The church is not a business, and Jesus Christ is not just a product. The church is more than a business, and Jesus Christ will do more for an individual than any product. Consequently, it is not just as important for the church to get its message out—it is *more* important.

Recognizing that there is a variety of people in the world and that different people respond in different ways, here are some of the methods churches can use to communicate effectively:

1. *Word-of-mouth.* This is probably the most popular and the most effective means through which people hear about a church. But it is only one of many ways.

2. *The church sign.* Many churches rely on this method of advertisement the most. Depending on the location and the visibility of the church, a sign can be a helpful way to let people know about the church. But it must be perpendicular to the road and large enough to read. I just consulted a church that is getting a computerized message sign. Why not? We have the greatest message ever.

3. *The telephone book.* It is surprising how many people look in the telephone book for a church. This is true not only of the white pages but also of the yellow pages. Many churches provide a Web site on the Internet. This avenue of exposure is becoming increasingly useful and effective.

4. *Mass mailing.* Many churches use the direct-mail approach. If your church decides to use this method, it is helpful to employ a professional firm to ensure quality material. Don't make the mistake of thinking that one mass

mailing will make an impact. If you plan to send only one mailing, you should probably not send any.

5. *Radio.* Most churches are surprised at how easy it is to get a public service announcement on many radio stations. Paid, professionally produced advertising from Christian churches is so rare that it could have a tremendous effect, especially in cities with a population of thirty thousand or less.

6. *Newspapers.* Articles are especially helpful in small-town newspapers. These papers are always looking for material. A photograph especially helps to draw the reader's attention. In larger cities, newspapers with big circulations are generally not responsive to church news.

7. *Billboards.* Billboard advertising can be fairly expensive unless a congregation has a member with property on a main highway, and the church owns the billboard. State and local laws are becoming stricter about billboards. But in many areas, a properly placed billboard can still be an effective means of advertising for a church. It is especially helpful in conjunction with a special event in the congregation.

8. *Cable television.* In many cities with fewer than fifty thousand people, cable television provides an affordable opportunity for a church to have an outreach ministry. But do not plan to broadcast a worship service unless you want to reach only shut-in members of your church or your denomination. To reach others, you will have to tell stories or present drama or provide commentary on events or situations relevant to the community.

9. *Information in local hotels and motels.* Many hotels and motels have a directory or provide an opportunity for a church to place information in the materials that guests receive when they check in. Churches that are serious about providing a service for those who are visiting will provide not only worship service information but also a map, and perhaps even a telephone number that can be called for "limo service" to the church.

10. *Posters.* Laundry facilities, shopping centers, drug stores, and many other establishments provide bulletin boards for community-oriented events. This can be a helpful strategy for special events and special ministries that the church offers.

11. *Welcomers.* Those who move into the community can be welcomed through welcome agencies or other contacts made with new residents. Some utility companies or real estate companies will provide names of new residents.

12. *Special events.* Some churches have special events away from the church. These may include a choir singing Christmas carols at a shopping mall, a free car wash for nonmembers, or a booth at a local county fair. The important part of this strategy is to invite individuals to hear the gospel and to get the names and addresses of as many prospects as possible. Some churches use the strategy of giving away a free Bible (for which people register) as a way of obtaining contacts.

13. *Open-house missions.* These special events occur when a church plans several days designated as an open house. The church invites a special speaker and advertises heavily to the community. The church encourages members to bring unchurched friends and relatives. These events usually not only provide contacts for prospective members but often reactivate members who have become delinquent. A variation of this is a Friend Day, on which members are encouraged to bring a friend.

14. *Special festivals at the church.* Unfortunately, most bazaars or other activities are for the purpose of making money. But with a proper mission mind-set, churches may present many of the same events grounded in a mission motive rather than a money motive. An example is a congregation in a fairly wealthy suburb of a large metropolitan area that has an antique boutique every year. If names and addresses are obtained, such events can provide opportunities for contacts within the community.

DIFFERENT STROKES FOR DIFFERENT FOLKS

God has placed his church in a pluralistic world filled with a beautiful variety of people. Each person has the same basic need: Jesus Christ, his forgiveness, and new life in him.

For Jesus to reach these people, a variety of methods, styles, music, programs, and strategies of outreach is necessary. Each local church cannot provide enough variety to reach every group at once. Stewardship of the gospel will require wise choices for the deployment of resources. But the general principle is that most churches would be more effective by adding some variety. The church must burn with passion and demonstrate flexibility to reach people for Jesus Christ. That passion burns not only for the immediate community but also to the ends of the earth. The local church must become not only a mission but also a world outreach center as it grows, multiplying churches around the world.

Discussion Questions

1. How would you describe the "culture" of your church? What kinds of people are attracted to this culture? What kinds of people are not?

2. Can you clearly differentiate between unity and conformity? Which predominates in your church? Do you need to make adjustments in the balance between the two? To what end?

3. Do you make a conscious effort to provide different worship experiences for different people groups? If yes, is it effective? In what ways might you expand or improve your options?

4. In what ways do you communicate the message of your church to your community? Are they consciously directed and goal oriented, or have they just become

traditional approaches that have been perpetuated without expectations or measurable results?

5. What efforts have you made to discover why people visit your church? Why do they return (or not return)? Why do they seek membership? Why do they become disciples, or why do they eventually drift out the back door?

6. Discuss the pros and cons of a church that ministers to the spiritual and other needs of a tightly targeted group of people (homogeneity) versus one that embraces a diversity of people (heterogeneity). Which are you? Which can, or should, you be? Does a church that includes a preponderance of similar kinds of people have more or less potential for moving the church to action?

10

THE WORLD OUTREACH CENTER

Every church, in a sense, is an outreach center. Just as Jesus said that he had not come to condemn the world but to save it, God has called his people to reach the world, not just the neighborhood. The Great Commission is to make disciples of all people groups. At the time of his ascension the Lord called his people to be witnesses to the ends of the world. Not only is this aspect of church life important for the fulfillment of the Great Commission; it is also part of the mix that moves the church to action. It is not just a teaching or an emphasis; it is a posture toward world evangelism. Reaching the world for Jesus Christ is not merely an annual theme or a denominational program. It must become a passion and an activity for the local church. Every Christian, whether one sent to foreign lands or a lifelong member of the local church, is a vital link in the support network that God has called together for the purpose of world mission.

HORIZONTAL HORIZONS WITH VERTICAL VALUES

Christian growth in the life of a disciple includes growing in an awareness of stewardship, understanding the Bible, identifying spiritual gifts, training and witnessing, and developing a prayer life. It also includes becoming a world Christian.

World Christians are conscious of the worldwide scope of the mission of the church and of their particular part in that mission. They are concerned about the activity of the Christian church in every part of the world. They see beyond their own little communities and view the world through a special lens: a concern for world evangelization. They see current events in light of the effect they will have on the cause of Christ and whether they will further or hinder the work of the Great Commission. For example, to world Christians, events like the opening of China, famine in Africa, tensions in the Middle East, or a summit meeting between superpowers have more significance than the political and social implications.

World Christians are informed about the international aspects of outreach with the gospel. Three special resources can help a person become an informed world Christian. The magazine *World Evangelization* is available from the Lausanne Committee for World Evangelization (2531 Nina Street, Pasadena, California 91107). *Strategies for Today's Leader* is a publication that provides practical help for church leaders and active Christians, with a focus on evangelization. It is available from The Church Doctor ministries (P.O. Box 145, Corunna, Indiana 46730). A third resource would be your own denominational publication. Most church mission boards have a resource magazine or newsletter that tells about the mission activities of the denomination.

World Christians pray for world evangelization. They pray for the missionaries who are on the front lines of activity in many lands, usually far away from homes and relatives. Often at great personal sacrifice, missionaries work cross-culturally to bring the gospel to areas where the Christian church is just gaining a foothold. World Christians pray for countries and continents and people groups yet unreached by the gospel. They also pray for ministries that are geared to promote world evangelization.

World Christians also participate through monetary support for world evangelization. Money is desperately needed in so many ministries that are committed to the fulfillment of the Great Commission. World Christians want to invest not only in the work of ministry at home but also in the worldwide efforts of the Christian church.

Laser Christianity

It may sound shocking, but the potential is great for the fulfillment of the Great Commission in this generation. God has provided a worldwide mix that, if properly employed, motivated, and focused, could perhaps complete the task of world evangelization in a matter of decades. Some believe that it could happen in the twenty-first century.

This mix includes an enormous force of workers. There are more missionaries in the Christian church worldwide than ever before. More people are directly committed to the fulfillment of the Great Commission than ever before. Some of the greatest thinkers and hardest workers in the Christian church have been charged and motivated for the worldwide mission effort.

Second, the potential financial resources available are unlike those of any time in history. Enormous amounts of wealth remain untapped, especially in the West. All too often Christian causes operate on a shoestring. It is only necessary to inform Christians of the need and to motivate them to use the opportunity for world evangelization. The money is there.

Third, God has provided great blessings in the technology that can be used for world evangelization. Computers, word processing, air travel, satellite communications, and many other modern conveniences can aid the strategy to deploy Christian workers to unreached people groups to the ends of the earth.

The primary need is for focus. A laser beam focuses a high concentration of light. The light of Jesus Christ and his people in the world today is enough for that light to shine throughout the world as the Lord intends (1 Tim. 2:3-4). It just needs to be focused. One candle only emits a little bit of light in the darkness, but many candles . . .

Years ago when I was at a Christian youth conference in Texas, tens of thousands of Christian young people packed the stadium one night to hear Billy Graham. My wife and I were seated on the artificial turf on the fifty-yard line right in the center of the stadium. At the end of the evening one person lit a match and touched it to the wick of a candle, and as the light spread and multiplied, the lights of the stadium were extinguished. The light of tens of thousands of candles was shining. It looked like daylight. The potential for the light was there all the time. All it took was willing Christians and an organized method of spreading the light. The need for world evangelization today is that Christians be organized and released to focus their resources for the Great Commission.

Laser Christianity starts at the local church. It starts with people who are concerned, informed, prayerful, and supportive. Furthermore, discipleship that includes the development of world-mission Christians helps discover those who are called to such a ministry. It will locate those people whom God wants to spend their lives as missionaries. It will find those whom God will use as workers for sending agencies. He will help find and employ people to work in areas such as telecommunications and computer technology. They will dedicate their lives for the cause of world mission.

There are many retired or semi-retired people who need to be challenged, motivated, and directed toward areas in the Christian church where there is a crying need for career volunteers. Career volunteers are unpaid, full-time "employees" who dedicate their lives for the work of the Great Commission. Some denominations use retirees to help build small church buildings at a great savings to the church. Some career volunteers are needed in the African mission field. Others are needed in agencies that help stimulate world evangelization.

For example, Bob, who had recently retired, and his wife moved halfway across the United States so he could become a full-time worker at a parachurch ministry. He worked for nothing—no pay, no fringe benefits. Bob can be an inspiration to many people. There are many who have years of experience. Like Bob, they have often spent a lifetime as active laypeople in a Christian church. There are many retired people who need to be needed. They need to be challenged to consider what Bob calls his "last religious fling."

If more Christians of all ages can be challenged to focus their energies, they will make a tremendous difference for world evangelization. More people will be reached for Jesus Christ sooner.

As this emphasis becomes a part of the life of the local church, it is not just an asset to world evangelization. It is also part of the mix that moves the church to action for discipleship and mission.

A Sending Church

Your church can become a congregation that sends support, people, and prayers for the cause of world evangelization. A growing number of churches support their own missionary family or families. This personalized mission support is gratifying to the members, and it helps bring the cause of mission closer to home.

A church can adopt a people group. Every year the Mission Advanced Research Center (MARC), a division of World Vision, publishes an updated list of all the unreached people groups in the world. This publication, called *Unreached Peoples*, is available from MARC (919 Huntington Drive, Monrovia, California 91016). As Christians discover more about unreached people groups, they can pray for them.

If your church is going to be healthy and vital, it needs to support financially and to pray for your denominational agencies and their efforts. It is also important for your church to continue to support and pray for independent agencies around the world.

God blesses the church that is part of his plan. That's part of the mix for a church that wants to move forward in discipleship and mission.

Discussion Questions

1. What does "outreach" imply in your church? Is it confined to family, friends, neighbors, community, inactive members, nation, denominational mission support, English-speaking peoples? Does it extend to personal involvement in reaching all peoples in all places?

2. Given the present and potential resources at your disposal, how can you best develop "world Christians" at your church? Does this demand a wider or narrower focus than now exists?

3. Formulate a strategy for communicating, targeting, and supporting one or more specific areas of world outreach in your church.

EPILOGUE: COUNTING THE COST

Whenever God's kingdom has grown, it has cost something. It cost Jesus his life. It cost his disciples their lives.

Down through the centuries, Christian leaders have sacrificed much for the cause of Jesus Christ. In fact, rapid Kingdom growth necessitates sacrifice.

In South Korea it is common for Christians to stop at church on their way to work and pray for their pastors and leaders, and for the gospel to reach the hearts and lives of their countrymen. God hears and answers prayer. Today Korea is one of the countries where Christianity is growing rapidly.

The health and vitality of the local church and the growth of God's kingdom have always had a price tag. Do you really want to see your church moved to action? Do you sincerely want God's people to be involved in a life of discipleship and to develop a vision for mission? Jesus had a warning. He said that before one builds a tower, one should sit down and count the cost (Luke 14:28-30). Activating a stalled congregation is what God does. But God does it through people who sacrifice much time, energy, and money.

God promises that he will provide for all the needs of those who seek his kingdom first (Matt. 6:28-33). Whenever God presents a challenge, he also makes a promise: God will fulfill our needs.

When Jesus gave the Great Commission, he did so from a position of authority. He said, "All authority in heaven and on earth has been given to me" (Matt. 28:18). Then he presented the challenge of the Great Commission to make disciples of all peoples everywhere. Finally, he closed with a promise: "Surely I am with you always, to the very end of the age" (v. 20). He promised his presence. And at Pentecost he gave his power so that his people—empowered by the Holy Spirit—could be his witnesses to the ends of the earth. That is life's greatest adventure. That is the church in action.